# Not a Tame Lion

## THE SPIRITUAL LEGACY OF C.S. LEWIS

## TERRY W. GLASPEY

### GENERAL EDITOR, GEORGE GRANT

LEADERS IN ACTION SERIES

Highland Books

Not a Tame Lion:
The Spiritual Legacy of C.S. Lewis

ISBN 0-9645396-7-5
Copyright © 1996 by Terry W. Glaspey
General Editor: George Grant

Published by Highland Books
229 South Bridge Street
P.O. Box 254
Elkton, MD 21922-0254
Tel. (410) 392-5554
Send requests for information to the above address.

Cover Photo courtesy of Arthur P. Strong, Sweden.

**Printed in the United States of America.**

*For Darren Jacobs,*
*"Aslan is on the move"*

"I wonder," said Jewel, "whether Aslan might not come though all the stars foretold otherwise. He is not the slave of the stars but their Maker. Is it not said in all the old stories that he is not a tame lion?"

"Well said, well said," cried the King. "Those are the very words: not a tame lion. It comes in many tales."

*–The Last Battle*

# TABLE OF CONTENTS

# FOREWORD

## by George Grant

*A*ccording to the great English pundit and critic, Samuel Johnson, a leader is "a man who bears in his life both the most tangible and intangible qualities of heart and mind and flesh. Best we study these well."

What is it exactly that makes a man a great leader? What constitutes genuine leadership? What character traits are necessary to steer men and nations into the way they should go? How may we train young people to become such leaders as they ought to be—and we need them to be? How are we to "study well" that which is both "the most tangible and intangible" simultaneously?

These are particularly relevant questions in this difficult day of profound leaderlessness. There can be little doubt that we are the most over-managed yet under-led generation in recent memory—thus, our great imperious task is to somehow buck the trend and wrestle with such questions.

In this penetrating analysis of the life, work, and thought of C. S. Lewis, Terry Glaspey not only wrestles with those questions, he affords us with some surprising answers. His insight into the remarkable continuing influence of this man is likely to redefine our conception of true leadership.

C. S. Lewis, after all, was not a politician—indeed, he was practically apolitical. He was not a man of military prowess or valor. He was not the progenitor of a new social movement or philosophical school. He was not a populist orator or community organizer. In fact, his quiet life as a traditional English don hardly measures up to our peculiar notions of what it takes to be a leader—which may well help to explain our current dismal estate.

Despite all appearances, Lewis was undoubtedly a great leader. And as Terry Glaspey makes all too evident, he is the sort of leader we ought to look to as a model in our own day.

My introduction to Lewis, like that of so many others, came through his fiction. I had enthusiastically read the works of his great friend J. R. R. Tolkien and was hungry for more of the same. At first, as I read the *Chronicles of Narnia,* I was rather disappointed. I had expected the same kind of epic drama that *The Lord of the Rings* had pioneered. But my disappointment quickly dissipated. I began to see that the imagination of Lewis was as solitary and substantial as that of his Inkling peer—and in fact, I found it to be even more satisfying in many ways.

I went on to read everything that Lewis wrote—as well as everything about Lewis, and everything about all those in the Lewis circle—that I could possibly get my hands on. And there was plenty to get my hands on—an entire cottage industry had grown up around this quiet, unpretentious literary man. Gradually, imperceptibly, I discovered that he had begun to reshape my thinking, realign my priorities, and redefine the parameters of my fledgling worldview—as he had so many others. Lewis had become for me, a leader. And so he remains to this day: "He being dead still speaketh" (Hebrews 11:4).

The evidence of one of the most brilliant creative minds of the twentieth century, his wide-ranging work continues to cross over all literary, philosophical, and religious boundaries.

A world-renowned university scholar of medieval literature at both Oxford and Cambridge, he was simultaneously able to write and lecture in such clear, direct language that ordinary men and women were fully able to comprehend truths he extolled. And, of course, he was a prolific author of such compelling classic masterpieces of English prose as *The Screwtape Letters*, *The Problem of Pain*, *Experiment in Criticism*, *Pilgrim's Regress*, *The Discarded Image*, *Mere Christianity*, and the beloved *Chronicles of Narnia*.

As I began to think about the men I believed were the best exemplars of substantive leadership and public virtue who I would profile in this series, I never had any doubts that Lewis would be among them. In the pantheon of heroism, his name ranks high. After reading this volume, I trust you will see just why.

In *Not a Tame Lion*, Terry Glaspey allows us a clear view of the character of this extraordinarily gifted man who believed that his sharp mind and rich imagination were accompanied by a sense of responsibility to the wider world. Thus, this book demonstrates why, a generation after his death, Lewis continues to be numbered among our best-selling authors and our most influential thinkers.

Herein are most assuredly "both the most tangible and intangible qualities of heart and mind and flesh."

It is sage counsel that exhorts, "Best we study these well."

# ACKNOWLEDGMENTS

Special thanks, as always, to my wife Sally and my daughters, Emma and Kathryn, for encouragement, perspective, love, and for putting up with my long hours in front of the computer. You bring much joy to my life.

Thanks to George Grant, for giving me the opportunity to contribute to this distinguished series of biographical studies and for his tireless efforts on behalf of the Kingdom.

Thanks to all the wonderful people at Great Christian Books who contributed to the process of creating this book, most especially Dean Andreola, Heather Armstrong, Nancy Drazga, and Karen Taylor. It has been such a pleasure to work with you all.

Thanks to those friends who share my love and enthusiasm for Lewis' books, especially Darren Jacobs, Carolyn McCready, Steve Miller, Ken Taylor, Trudy Kutz, Kim Moore, and Greg Spencer.

And thanks to those scholars and writers who have sought to keep Lewis' message fresh for our time, especially Sheldon Vanauken, Peter Kreeft, Walter Hooper, Corbin Scott Carnell, Humphrey Carpenter, William Griffin, George Sayer, and Peter Schakel. Also to Christopher W. Mitchell and the fine people at the Wade Center at Wheaton College, who strive to keep Lewis scholarship alive.

Let us go through the wardrobe door together.

# INTRODUCTION

*I* first encountered C. S. Lewis at a particularly difficult time in my early Christian experience. The failings of the church left me questioning the reality of the faith I had embraced. I was struck by the dissonance between words and action. The church seemed to lay the greatest stress on issues hardly addressed by our Lord, and seemed to largely ignore His sometimes radically uncomfortable demands. My disillusionment was heightened by the general unwillingness of most of the Christians I knew to really deal with life's most vexing questions. Instead of being challenged to engage my mind in pursuit of the truth, I was given poorly-thought-out formulaic answers and told that to question these conclusions was a sign of spiritual immaturity. I was almost prepared to surrender my faith in disgust. Perhaps, I thought, I had been taken for a ride…

And then I met Lewis. Well, not the man himself, but the man as I found him in the pages of his books. Here was a man who had engaged in a quest for answers and had, indeed, found some. It was not so much the content of his argument that was a help at this crucial time in my life, but the encouragement to search because there were answers to be found. It was also the winsome, creative and intelligent personality that radiated from between the lines of his writing. If such a man could wholeheartedly embrace Christianity, then perhaps it deserved a more careful look than I had yet given it.

Within a couple of years I read everything I could find by Lewis. Not only did he deepen my understanding of the Christian worldview, but he also helped me see God with fresh eyes, helping Him to emerge from the mists of my upbringing into the radiant light of fullness. I came to love Lewis' portrayal of Christ in Aslan, the great lion from *The Chronicles of Narnia*. (I have since had the pleasure of sharing these books aloud with my children.) Here was a God who did not fit into my comfortable preconceptions or a denominational box, a God upon whom I could not press my personal agendas. For as one of the characters says of him, "He is not a tame lion."

Neither was Lewis a "tame lion," whose message could be comfortably summed up under a single label. He often surprises his readers or makes them uncomfortable. He was not a theological liberal, but neither did his views square with fundamentalism. He was not the cold professorial type portrayed in the film "Shadowlands," but neither was he a man who wore his emotions on his sleeve. He was a man who believed that God had given him a mind and common sense, and expected him to make use of these gifts, but it was in his flights of literary fantasy that his deepest perceptions of God were birthed.

In a day when our religious options seem limited to a closed-minded confidence that we are the exclusive purveyors of truth, or to a faith more concerned with being up-to-date than being faithful to God's revelation, Lewis brings us a fresh vision. Paradoxically, the freshness of his approach is based upon his intellectual commitment to tradition. His continued relevance is based upon that commitment and on his understanding of the human predicament—a predicament that is intellectual and moral, as well as spiritual. Lewis points the way out of this predicament, but it is not an easy way. It demands submission to God's authority, moral discipline, and integrity of action. His is a message for a time such as this.

This book is written with the average reader in mind. There are many fine scholarly biographies and literary studies of Lewis in print. In fact, the study of Lewis has become a minor industry in Christian academic circles. He is certainly among the most quoted of modern Christians and one who is appreciated across denominational and philosophical lines. And yet, many believers are only familiar with a small number of his writings. This is a shame, because there is such richness to be found throughout his books. What I have attempted to do in this book is to give the reader a sense of Lewis' major accomplishments by providing a brief look at his life and a summary of some of his major ideas. But this book can not even begin to plumb the full riches of Lewis' work. My hope is that this book will become the impetus for further exploration by the reader.

As we explore Lewis' life and thought, I have tried to let him speak for himself as much as possible. He is a writer whose insight is so well balanced with his wit, that he always says it better than I could paraphrase it. If the result of reading this book is to awaken a hunger to read some of his books for yourself, then I have accomplished my task.

# Chronology of C. S. Lewis' Life

1951, Death of Janie Moore.
1952, Published *Mere Christianity*.
1953, First meeting with Joy Davidman Gresham.
1954, Given chair of Medieval and Renaissance Literature at Cambridge University.
1955, Published autobiography, *Surprised by Joy*.
1956, Published *Till We Have Faces*.
1956, Married Joy Davidman Gresham, who was dying of cancer.
1957, Joy's cancer goes into miraculous remission.
1959, Joy suffers relapse.
1960, Death of Joy Lewis.
Published *The Four Loves*.
1961, Published *A Grief Observed*.
1963, Death of C. S. Lewis (November 22).

# C. S. Lewis:
## His Life

# September 28, 1931

The morning was cold and a heavy fog loitered over the damp grass. It was causing some second thoughts at the Lewis home, just outside Oxford, about the planned trip to the Whipsnade Zoo, some forty miles away. C. S. Lewis (known to all his friends as "Jack") and his brother Warren were all for braving the elements, but their companions, Janie Moore and her daughter Maureen, hesitated. At last it was decided that the brothers would get a head start on Warren's motorcycle and the women would follow in the car. They planned to meet in the town of Whipsnade.

Warren mounted the motorcycle and Jack took his place in the low-slung sidecar. They fired up the cycle and disappeared into the thick mist, roaring into the cold morning air. Alone with his thoughts, Jack Lewis braced himself against the biting wind and considered the issue which had so dominated his thoughts lately: who was Jesus Christ? Could he accept the claim that Christ was God incarnate?

Just beyond the small town of Thame, the fog lifted and the bright sunshine broke through the swirling mists. The air was crisp and fresh as the trees and towns zoomed past them.

Shortly before one o'clock they cruised into the town of Whipsnade and pulled off the road to await the arrival of the women. They spread themselves out on the grass and opened a bottle of dark English beer, which they shared.

They waited, growing anxious and hungry, because their lunch was in the car. Finally, about 2:20, the car appeared, its passengers somewhat irritable and short-tempered. There had been problems with the car and their mechanic had over-filled the tires, making it impossible to drive any faster than 15 mph. Warren commiserated, saying that the same thing had happened to him recently. An abundant lunch, however, helped lift the level of stress and set a new tone for the day.

Everyone enjoyed themselves thoroughly, though Warren complained that the zoo was a bit of a disappointment, as it housed too few animals. The consensus was that the bears were most definitely the highlight of the day, especially a bulky brown bear whom Jack christened "Bultitude." He wanted to adopt it and take it home to Headington, he jested with a wry smile. (In fact, he would later give this name to a large bear that played a key role in his science-fiction novel, *That Hideous Strength*.) When it came time for the zoo to close, everyone packed up and headed home in high spirits.

To all outward appearances, this was a very ordinary day, a day like any other. And yet it would be remembered as a most momentous day in the life of C. S. Lewis, for it was a day of decision. As he later wrote in his autobiography: "When we set out I did not believe that Jesus Christ is the Son of God, and when we reached the zoo I did."[1] Lewis' conversion, the culmination of a lifelong journey toward the truth, would give new direction and purpose to his life resulting in the writing of many books which had a profound influence both on his own time, and on generations to follow. By his words and his life, Lewis demonstrated the power of a life touched by a deep intellectual commitment to the truth of the Gospel, and of an imagination energized by the glory of the Christian vision of reality.

# HERITAGE

*C*live Staples Lewis was born on a wintry day in Belfast, Ireland on November 29, 1898, the second child of Albert and Florence Lewis. His mother, Florence Hamilton, or "Flora" as she was known to intimates, was a highly intelligent woman. She had earned an honors degree in mathematics at Queens University in Belfast, an uncommon achievement for a woman at that time. The Hamilton family tree was made up of a string of clergymen. Flora's grandfather and great-grandfather had both been clergymen, the latter attaining the office of bishop. Her father, Thomas Hamilton, followed in their footsteps, becoming a vicar in the Church of Ireland. Thomas was a memorable personality, who combined a gift for eloquence with a pugnacious and uncompromising spirit. He was a man of deep piety, though far from an ascetic, for he dearly enjoyed his food and drink. His other great love was his daughter Flora, who was the dearest thing to his heart, and his desire was for her to make the best of marriages.

In 1894, after a long courtship by a very determined Albert Lewis, she finally consented to marry him. He had persistently pursued her and finally won her favor. Probably his skill as an orator and a debater did much to help him win her hand. Albert's grandfather had been a Welsh farmer, while Richard Lewis, Albert's father, was a self-made man, rising by stages through his profession until he became a partner in an engineering and manufacturing firm. An avid writer of theological essays, Richard would often read them to his co-workers during the evening shift. Sometimes he would make up fantastical stories for the amusement of his children. Clearly, storytelling was in the Lewis blood.

Albert inherited a great deal of his father's drive and creativity, but seemed destined to fail to realize his full potential. Educated at Lurgan College under the brilliant young headmaster, W. T. Kirkpatrick (who would later tutor his sons), he showed great promise and dreamed of eventually taking a seat in the House of Commons. Instead, he spent most of his career as a prosecuting solicitor in the Belfast police courts. Here, his talents at debate and oratory came to full flower, and though he never achieved his full ambition, his skill and honesty won him respect in the judicial community. Albert had a rich sense of humor, and was known for his mastery of the anecdotal tale and for his seemingly inexhaustible fund of improbable stories, which he referred to as "wheezes."

Though Albert and Flora did not make the most romantic of attachments, they held in common a love of beauty and good books and found each other's companionship most agreeable. They settled in a house just outside of Belfast, where some of their sons' earliest memories would be formed.

# A Romantic Temperament

*A*s the slanting rain fell outside the windows of their home, Lewis and his brother Warren (or "Warnie" as he was affectionately known) passed the long wet Belfast days inside. The miserable weather and their mother's fear that her sons might contract an infectious disease from being caught in a rain shower meant that the two Lewis boys spent a disproportionate percentage of their youth indoors. With little to entertain them but their imaginations, they set to work with their pencils, chalk, paints and paper.

Though separated by three years of age, the two boys became and remained the very best of friends, even into adulthood. They found immense pleasure in each other's company and in the creative pursuits which they shared in common. Lewis' brilliance and intellectual acuity were obvious from an early age, sometimes taking the form of precociousness. When he was four years old Lewis decided, as many children do, that he did not like his given name, Clive. One day, he simply announced that his name was "Jacksie," and refused to answer to any other. The name stuck, soon shortened to "Jack," the name by which he was known to all his close friends for the rest of his life.

Lewis was, by his own admission, of a romantic temperament from his earliest days. The green hills of Castlereagh, visible from the nursery window, were only the first in a series of sights and events that inspired the romantic vision. "They were not very far off but they were, to children, quite unobtainable. They taught me longing– Sehnsucht; made me for good or ill, and before I was six years old, a votary of the Blue Flower."[2] The "blue flower" image is drawn from a book by the German romantic poet and novelist, Novalis, who used it as a symbol for a sort of transcendent inkling of supernatural joy, a longing to be merged into the very mystery of things. Though he could not yet express it in words, these are the kinds of feelings that haunted the young Lewis.

The same sense of inconsolable longing was activated by the memory, while standing one morning in the garden, of a toy garden his brother had given to him in the nursery, a garden in a biscuit tin, filled with moss, stones, twigs and small flowers. It also rose unbidden in the reading of a Beatrix Potter story, *Squirrel Nutkin*, and in the reading of a translation of an old Icelandic epic. Analyzing these experiences, Lewis found that their common quality was "an unsatisfied desire which is itself more desirable than any other satisfaction."[3] At the time, this was the closest thing to a religious experience he was to have, since the family religion of his childhood meant little to him. This experience, similar to that described by William Wordsworth and Thomas Traherne, was in reality a desire for, and a sense of, the presence of God, though only later in life would this realization dawn upon him.

Interestingly, little of this romantic sense can be found in Lewis' childhood writing. In those long hours in their rooms, Jack and Warnie imagined a land called "Boxen," where chivalrous frogs came to the aid of King Bunny of Animal–Land or engaged in various political machinations. The numerous stories the brothers wrote and illustrated about the history of Boxen are surprisingly prosaic, lacking in the poetry, romance, and invention which mark Jack's adult work. Instead, the stories became part of a mammoth game of creating an entire integrated history of this imaginary place, complete with chronologies, maps and lists of rulers.

As other boys, Jack and Warnie loved the outdoors and made full use of the days they were allowed outside. They would ride their bikes and explore the neighborhood. They also treasured the frequent trips, by train, to the sea and enjoyed splashing about in the waves. These holidays at the beach were fondly remembered, but also reveal something about the nature of Albert Lewis. Their father was a man totally immersed in his job, sometimes to the detriment of his family. He could be cold and remote, often distracted and morose, and easily bored when away from the routines of his office. Warren recalls: "I can still see him on his occasional flying visits to the seaside, walking moodily up and down the beach, and every now and then giving a heartrending yawn and pulling out his watch."[4] His father's emotional ups and downs taught Jack a distrust of emotions that would stay with him throughout his life.

In 1907 the family moved a short distance to a grand old house called "Little Lea." Though not in the best of repair, it was full of charm and mystery. It was a huge sprawling edifice, with an attic running nearly the full length of the house and tunnels running along under the ridge tiles on the roof. This immense attic expanse became a private place of refuge for the boys. Here, in secret, they could write, draw and add to the fund of their Boxen legends. It was a place where their imaginations could flourish. As Lewis wrote in his autobiography:

> *I am the product of long corridors, empty sunlit*
> *rooms, upstairs indoor silences, attics explored*
> *in solitude, distant noises of gurgling cisterns*
> *and pipes, and the noise of wind under the*
> *tiles.*[5]

But immense changes were to occur over the next few years which would destroy this idyllic existence.

The first was when Warren was sent off to school at Wynyard House, leaving Jack alone in his secret world. Although he continued to develop the Boxen stories, Jack began to spend an increasing amount of time reading. The book-lined corridors of "Little Lea" offered many volumes to feed his imagination and satisfy his ever-growing desire to read. Many of the books he read at this time would be considered very advanced for his age, but he digested and enjoyed such books as *Gulliver's Travels*, the E. Nesbit stories, and even *Paradise Lost*.

A more cataclysmic change was to occur in early 1908 when Flora Lewis consulted with doctors about the tiredness, headaches and loss of appetite which she was experiencing. The doctors diagnosed it as abdominal cancer and operated on her. Living under a regimen of nurses, medications and the emotional convulsions of his father, Jack felt the pain of oncoming tragedy:

> *We lost her gradually as she was gradually*
> *withdrawn from our life into the hands of*
> *nurses and delirium and morphia, and as our*
> *whole existence changed into something alien*
> *and menacing, as the house became full of*
> *strange smells and midnight noises and sinister*
> *whispered conversations.*[6]

She died on August 23, 1908. This was one of a series of tragedies that Albert experienced that year. Earlier in the year, his father had died, and ten days after Flora's death, his beloved brother Joseph died. By this time Albert Lewis had already withdrawn deeply into his own grief, becoming moody and distant. Lacking the confidence that he could raise the boys on his own, he determined to send Jack to Wynyard, where he could join Warnie. It marked the end of an era in Jack's life:

> *With my mother's death all settled happiness, all that was tranquil and reliable, disappeared from my life. There was to be much fun, many pleasures, many stabs of Joy; but no more of the old security. It was sea and islands now; the great continent had sunk like Atlantis.*[7]

# WYNYARD AND CHERBOURG

$\mathcal{F}$ollowing his mother's death, Jack was abruptly sent off to boarding school in England. It was, according to Lewis, a nightmarish experience, so much so that in his autobiography he referred to the school as "Belsen." As Warren later put it, "With his uncanny flair for making the wrong decision, my father had given us helpless children into the hands of a madman."[8]

It seems almost unthinkable that within two weeks of their mother's death, the two boys were sent away, not just to a new school, but a school that was in another country. Worst of all, the school to which they were sent was marked by cruelty and lack of feeling. Wanting to give his sons the advantage of a good public school education, one that would help them go on to Oxford or Cambridge, Albert took the worst of the advice he was given and sent the boys to Wynyard School in Watford. He never bothered to visit the school to see if was a good choice. If he had, he would surely have been taken aback by what he would have seen.

Wynyard was an unsanitary facility, with only one bathroom and a single washbasin for the entire student body.

Because of the limited facilities, each boy was allowed only one bath per week. The school had no playing fields and no library, the sick room was in a junk-strewn attic, and the playground was a patch of gravel. One of Warren's clearest memories was of the ever-present stench of the outdoor lavatory. He said that any sanitary inspector would unhesitatingly have condemned these places.

The headmaster of the school was a cruel tyrant named Robert Capron, who gave ready evidence of mental instability. He practiced discipline and enforced teaching by humiliating the boys and caning them in public. A boy could earn such dire punishment for as small an infraction as refusing to consume the infamously inedible food. Capron's teaching method was simple: memorization. His classes, therefore, were stultifyingly dull, emphasizing the rote acquisition of facts. Jack and Warren pleaded with their father to remove them. Jack later said that he learned absolutely nothing during his time there. "If I had been left for two years more, it would probably have sealed my fate as a scholar for good."[9]

Eventually their father listened to their pleas for help and transferred Jack to Campbell College in Belfast for half a term, after which he went on to Cherbourg in Malvern. Shortly thereafter, Wynyard was closed down.

While at Cherbourg, Lewis, like all young men, struggled with sexual thoughts and temptations and the attendant guilt. His method for overcoming this guilt was by a rejection of Christianity and its moral beliefs. He was using, of course, the well-traveled ploy of dealing with guilt by denying its reality. At this same time he came to develop a sophisticated taste for the arts and good writing. He also discovered the music of the great Romantic composer Richard Wagner and grew to love its transporting power and its "northernness," the quality of intense longing for the unknown which it evoked. In fact, one of his great life-long friendships was forged when he learned that Arthur Greeves, a neighbor boy of his own age, shared his delight in things "northern." Although they had been casual friends since childhood, it was the discovery of a shared love of Norse mythology that first drew them into close friendship. In 1933, Lewis was to refer to Arthur as "after my brother, my oldest and most intimate friend."[10] Over the years their correspondence was sufficient to fill a stout volume,[11] as they wrote lengthy letters on their shared love of books, the sexual temptations of adolescence, matters of faith, and the joys and struggles of family. Arthur was one of Jack's confidants throughout his life.

Jack was a precocious, if not a particularly great student. He ranked in the lower half of his class, for although he was quite gifted in literature and poetry, he was only mediocre in Greek and Latin and very poor in mathematics. The school had an excellent library, which he made use of at every opportunity, but he found little time for the reading and writing he had so come to love. His fellow students were more interested in games and cricket and eating than in actually learning anything.

Jack became increasingly disappointed with his school, with its bullying prefects, and with the education he was receiving. He begged his father to let him study with William Kirkpatrick, his father's old tutor, a man who had once helped Warnie at a time when his grades were plummeting.

# Learning to Learn

*A*s the train pulled up into the Great Bookham station, Jack prepared himself to meet his new tutor. His father often called him "dear Old Knock," and remembered him with great fondness. Jack expected a gentle, and embarrassingly sentimental old man. What he met instead was a tall, muscular and shabbily dressed gentleman with a mustache and sideburns on his wrinkled face. As they made their way to the tutor's house, Jack tried to make conversation by commenting on the countryside, saying that the scenery was much "wilder" than he had expected.

"Stop!" shouted Kirkpatrick with a vigor which caught Lewis by surprise. "What do you mean by wildness and what grounds had you for not expecting it?" When Jack replied that he did not know, Kirkpatrick told him that that was an unacceptable answer. Through vigorous questioning, Kirkpatrick demanded to know precisely what Lewis meant by his use of the word "wildness," and on what previous knowledge he had based his incorrect expectations. Fumbling for explanations, Jack only dug himself deeper into confusion, until Kirkpatrick was satisfied that he had uncovered Jack's ignorance. "Do you

not see, then, that you had no right to have any opinion whatever on the subject."[12]

Such was the teaching style of William T. Kirkpatrick, who
was to have such a profound influence on the life of C. S.
Lewis. He was a convinced rationalist, who loved to ferret out
inconsistencies and logical shortcomings. As Warren Lewis
once said, "You could not say something about the weather
without being pounced on."[13]

Kirkpatrick taught Lewis a love of argument, intellectual
disputation, the search for facts, and logical thinking. For
Kirkpatrick, opinions were of no use whatsoever; all that mat-
tered was deriving conclusions that were based on solid
reasoning. Lewis' time of study with the "Great Knock" would
be treasured throughout his life, for Kirkpatrick opened fully
the door to appreciation of the classics, to the philosophy of
the ancient world, and to the necessity of engaging the mind
fully in the pursuit of truth. The downside of Kirkpatrick's
influence was that it took Jack some years to learn to use his
analytical skills in a gentler manner. "The Christian virtue
that he found hardest to acquire was to suffer fools gladly; for
years he failed to realize that the Kirk treatment might upset
or offend."[14] In his early years, Lewis seemed to relish the
opportunity to thoroughly discredit the arguments of an opponent. In later years, he learned the talent of more gently
challenging false notions.

Kirkpatrick had high expectations and Jack found the
challenge inviting. Two days after his arrival at Bookham he
was put straight to work translating Homer, though he had
had no previous experience with the Epic dialect of the Greek
language. Kirkpatrick would read a few lines aloud and trans-
late them with a few comments, then leave Lewis with a
lexicon to continue the process. Lewis was a fast learner and
quickly memorized the necessary vocabulary. He worked at

translating Homer and other Greek classics until he could quite literally *think* in Greek. Kirkpatrick believed him to have the potential to be a brilliant translator. Jack also learned Italian and French, closely studied the classic works of the ancient world, and developed a taste for such writers as Milton, Spenser, Shelley, Bunyan, Chaucer, Swinburne and William Morris. "After a week's trial," he wrote to Arthur Greeves, "I have come to the conclusion that I am going to have the time of my life."[15] Probably the greatest gift which Kirkpatrick bestowed on Lewis was that of helping him learn how to teach himself. Throughout his life he never ceased to continue his education, exploring and mastering new ideas and subjects.

Kirkpatrick was a convinced atheist, and no doubt his influence on Lewis extended to the weakening of Lewis' already tenuous beliefs. Reading Frazer's *The Golden Bough* convinced Jack that all religion should be placed in the category of mythology. As he wrote to his close friend Arthur Greeves,

> *You ask me my religious view: you know, I think, that I believe in no religion. There is absolutely no proof for any of them, and from a philosophical standpoint Christianity is not even the best. All religions, that is all mythologies to give them their proper name, are merely man's own invention...*[16]

Interestingly, at the same time that Lewis was becoming more convinced of the falsity of religion, his fascination with Romanticism was growing. His letters to Arthur Greeves were filled with an enthusiasm for Norse mythology—the tales of Odin, Thor, and the other gods. During the time he lived and studied with Kirkpatrick, he kept up an elaborate correspondence with Greeves, the two sharing with each other their interests and adventures in reading.

A letter of March 7, 1916, documents an important moment in Lewis' life. In a bookstall in the train station at Great Bookham, he purchased a volume entitled *Phantastes*, by the Scottish writer George MacDonald. He devoured the book, completely entranced by the adventures of Anodos in a spiritual fairyland. He wrote to Greeves that it was "a great literary experience"[17] and that Greeves must find and read it. Later in life, Lewis recalled the reading of this book as not only a literary experience, but a spiritual one as well. At the time, however, Lewis sensed a certain quality that drew him to the book, though he could not define precisely what it was. Reflecting later, he wrote, "I did not yet know (and I was long in learning) the name of the new quality, the bright shadow... I do now. It was holiness."[18]

The young atheist, so confident in the world of materialism, could not suppress the longings that welled up in his heart and caused him to value things which his rationalism could not explain. "Such, then, was my position: to care for almost nothing but the gods and heroes, the garden of the Hesperides, Lancelot and the Grail, and to believe in nothing but atoms and evolution and military service."[19] But the first beginnings of a new view of life were birthed in his heart by MacDonald's strange and otherworldly tale. "That night my imagination was, in a certain sense, baptized; the rest of me, not unnaturally, took longer."[20]

# THE WOES OF WAR

*A*s the train pulled into the station, Jack's hopes rose. He had finally arrived at Oxford to embark on his new life as a student. He had long looked forward to the day when he would glimpse the dreaming spires of historic Oxford. Leaving the station, he was profoundly disappointed to find a series of rather run-down shops. This was nothing like the enchantment he had expected. As he walked on his disappointment grew. This was not what he had imagined. He stopped to ponder why this squalid town had such a reputation. Scratching his head, he chanced to look back over his shoulder.

At some distance he glimpsed the towers and spires, the beautiful magic of the architecture of the city of Oxford. He had inadvertently left the train station by the wrong exit and had found himself in the sprawling suburbs of Botley. Oxford lay in the other direction!

On finally arriving, Jack found Oxford all he had hoped it to be and settled down to his studies. This was a new world, full of intellectual challenge, history, and the beauties of architecture. It was a world for which young Jack seemed particularly suited and he entered it with relish. He enjoyed visiting the abundant bookshops, the magnificent libraries and the well-groomed grounds. It seemed almost a paradise on earth. To Arthur Greeves he enthused, "The place is on the whole absolutely ripping. If only you saw the quad on these moonlit nights with the long shadows lying half across the level, perfect grass and the tangle of spires & towers rising beyond in the dark!"[21]

This blissful time was cut short when Jack was called into service to fight in the First World War. He had spent fewer than eight weeks at Oxford, and the way the war was going, the odds were very strong that he might not return to England alive. Lewis was made a second lieutenant and attached to the Third Battalion of the Somerset Light Infantry. Before his posting to active duty, he was given one month's leave. He spent most of this time in the company of his roommate Edward "Paddy" Moore. Moore's mother Janie knew that the casualty rate at the front was very high, so she had moved to Oxford temporarily so that she could spend time with her son before he was sent to France. Rather than returning home, Jack spent his time with Paddy and Janie. He was immediately made to feel a part of the Moore family and quickly came to love Janie as a substitute mother. It was not long before his feelings were stirred to deeper levels. It became obvious to those who knew Jack at the time that he had become infatuated with her and fallen in love, despite the difference in their ages; she was 45, he only just shy of nineteen. This idyllic month came to an end when Lewis and Paddy Moore were sent to France for four short weeks of training and then shipped to the trenches.

November 29, 1917. It was an inauspicious way to spend one's nineteenth birthday: arriving on the battlefields of France where already so many of his generation had had their lives cut short by German bullets or bombs. The war effort had not gone well and Lewis joined his comrades in the cold and muddy trenches at the front lines. There they lived in constant fear of ammunition fire, disease and the ever-present rats. The death toll mounted as useless attacks upon the entrenched Germans were repulsed and young men breathed their last amongst the barbed wire in the no man's land between the two combatants' territories.

On April 15, 1918 Lewis was wounded during the Battle of Bernenchon by an English shell that exploded. Flying shrapnel pierced his body in three places. Warren, stationed in another part of France got wind of Jack's trouble and borrowed a bicycle to pedal fifty miles to be at his brother's side. As Warren reported to his father in a letter: "[A] shell burst close to where he was standing, killing a Sergeant, and lucky for 'IT' he only stopped three bits; one in the chest and two in the hands."[22]

In a way, Jack saw the fact that he had been wounded as something of a blessing. It may have been what preserved his life. As he wrote to his father from the hospital: "If I had not been wounded when I was, I should have gone through a terrible time. Nearly all my friends in the Battalion are gone."[23] His recovery was slow and he wrote to his father, asking him to come to visit him when he was transferred to a hospital in London. Although his father failed to materialize, he did receive a welcome visitor, Janie Moore.

Paddy Moore, like so many others, had died at the front. In fact, of the five boys who had visited the Moore residence in Oxford, only Jack remained. Jack had made a promise to Paddy to look after his mother in case anything happened to him on the battlefield. He was now only too glad to fulfill his pledge. For many years following, Jack lived with Janie and her daughter Maureen. Warren speaks of it as a mother and son relationship, but some biographers have suggested that it was a more intimate attachment. The exact nature of their relationship will probably never be entirely understood, but it seems clear that a deep affection between Jack and Janie lasted until her death.

# "The Trouble About God…"

*H*is health slowly recovered, and as the war ended, Jack returned to Oxford to begin his studies in earnest.

While recovering, Lewis had compiled a collection of his poems. In 1919, during his first year back at Oxford, the prestigious London publisher, Heinemann, released them under the title *Spirits in Bondage*. Published pseudonymously under the name Clive Hamilton, the book received some positive critical attention but sold rather poorly. The poems in this collection reflect something of Lewis' religious views at this time, not a strict atheism but a loose sort of pantheism. Traditional Christianity still held little attraction for him. To Arthur Greeves he wrote, "I believe in no God, least of all one that would punish me for the 'lusts of the flesh'; but I do believe that I have in me a spirit."[24] Part of the problem about belief in God was His inaccessibility: "The trouble about God is that He is like a person who never acknowledges one's letters and so, in time, you come to the conclusion either that He does not exist or that you have got the address wrong."[25]

During the summer of 1920 Janie Moore and her daughter moved to Oxford, where they rented a small house. Lewis pitched in on the rent, while he still lived at the college. Then in the summer of 1921, he moved out of his college lodgings and in with the Moores. Always having to scrape together a meager existence, Jack and the Moores occupied a succession of residences in Oxford. This made his lifestyle rather different from that of most of the professors and students, who were bachelors. Although it added financial stresses, life with the Moores lent a certain "ordinariness" to his existence. The simple homely domestic life was probably a better preparation for his future as a popular apologist and children's writer than if all his time had been spent with fellow academics. The "homeliness" and accessibility of many of Lewis' illustrations are certainly among the major qualities that have lent such popular appeal to his writings.

But many of Jack's friends, including his brother, wondered at what Jack saw in Mrs. Moore. The two never married and it is unclear whether they experienced anything beyond a mother and son relationship. Many biographers have speculated on the significance of their relationship, but it seems quite clear that if it had been sexual in nature that this would have been discontinued after Lewis' conversion because he held quite strong opinions against sexual promiscuity. Whatever their relationship was, it remained a puzzle to most of those who knew them. Warren writes:

> *She was a woman of very limited mind, and notably domineering and possessive by temperament. She cut down to a minimum his visits to his father, interfered constantly with his work, and imposed upon him a heavy burden of minor domestic tasks. In twenty years I*

> *never saw a book in her hands; her conversa-*
> *tion was chiefly about herself, and was*
> *otherwise a matter of ill-informed dogmatism:*
> *her mind was of a type that he found barely*
> *tolerable elsewhere.*[26]

"He is as good as an extra maid in the house," she once told a visitor in reference to Jack. In spite of the "distractions" of domestic life, Lewis accomplished a rare academic feat. He earned first class honors in three areas: Honor Mods (Greek and Latin classics), Greats (classical philosophy), and English language and literature.

Despite this accomplishment, it was still hard for him to find a teaching position. He applied for a classical lectureship at Reading, and for fellowships at St. John's and Trinity. All these positions were filled by others. While searching, he lived in near poverty. Only the financial assistance of his father kept him going. Because of the financial pressures of this time, he always had an understanding for the poor, was extremely generous with his money, and practiced a very frugal lifestyle. Finally, he was offered a temporary job at University College in Oxford, filling in for one year in the philosophy department. Although his knowledge of philosophy (especially ancient) was impressive, he did not feel that this was his strongest area of expertise. His lectures were sparsely attended and he felt himself to be less than a success at this job. He wrote in his diary:

> *On getting into bed I was attacked by a series of*
> *gloomy thoughts about professional and literary*
> *failure....I am haunted by fears for the future, as*
> *to whether I will ever get a job and whether I*
> *shall ever be able to write good poetry.*[27]

But the job did give him time to apply for all the fellowships that were offered. After many disappointments, he was offered a fellowship to teach English at Magdalen College in Oxford.

# THE RUMPLED PROFESSOR

*L*ewis loved the life of Oxford. When he did not eat with the Moores, he liked to take his meals in the dining hall, where sumptuous meals were included in the terms of his appointment. Then the tutors and professors would repair to the Senior Common Room for drinks and animated conversation.

Often, he was too busy to participate in this ritual, as he frequently had evening classes or a meeting with the "Koalbitars," a group of fellow academics who shared a love for the Old Norse myths and would gather together to read them in their original languages. J. R. R. Tolkien, who was to become one of Lewis' closest friends, was also a member of this group, whose name literally means "coal biters," an old Icelandic word for those who sit so closely by the fire that they appear to be biting the coals!

Jack's work at Oxford consisted mostly of the preparation of lectures and tutorials with his students. In his spare time he walked, wrote letters, and worked on a writing project that would eventually be published as *The Allegory of Love*.

Although he disliked tutorials, he was courteous and

patient, at least with those who did their work and who thought and expressed themselves clearly. Following the example of Kirkpatrick, he could be, early on, a harsh and demanding tutor, taking students to task for every ill usage of a word, careless remark or obfuscating dependence on technical jargon. In time, he developed a more gentle and sympathetic style, and is remembered fondly by those who studied under him. But he always had little patience for those who failed to take their work seriously.

Lewis' impatience with the intellectually lazy student arose from the fact that he hated to waste time, probably because his busy lifestyle left him with so little of it. Yet he made the most of the time he had. He read thoroughly and evidenced an amazing retention of what he read. He could bring forth from memory lengthy quotations from many authors with ease and accuracy. Derek Brewer, who once had Lewis as a tutor, remembers his amazing memory:

> *Lewis listened with extreme intentness, not I am all too sure, because of the fascination of my words, but because it was his duty. Once, in the middle of my essay, his phone rang. I stopped, and he answered it in the other room. When he returned after a five minute interruption, he repeated verbatim my last sentence as far as it had got. He had an astonishing verbatim memory and could repeat whole passages of prose to illustrate a point arising in a discussion. Given any line in Paradise Lost, he could continue with the following lines.*[28]

But such feats of memory were not performed for the attention of others. Lewis was never one for flash or show. "I love monotony," he once said. He was a man of simple tastes who enjoyed simple things: a walk in nature, fairy tales, playing with his cats and dogs. Known for his simple tastes, Lewis was not one to worry about fashion. All who knew him testify to a rather slovenly manner of dress. As a visitor to the Socratic Society of Oxford once described him:

> *[He wore] an old battered tweed sports coat. . .*
> *well-worn corduroy trousers, a patterned,*
> *well-washed shirt with a nondescript antique*
> *type tie. He was ruddy of complexion, radiating*
> *health, of substantial girth all over, and his*
> *eyes sparkled with mirth.*[29]

In general his appearance was, as one acquaintance said, that of a prosperous jolly farmer. Warren wrote that "Jack's clothes were a matter of complete indifference to him: he had the extraordinary knack of making a new suit look shabby the second time he wore it."[30]

But out of the mouth of this rather nondescript man came the most fascinating of ideas and observations. One observer spoke of his lecture style as exciting, noting that "vivid images and portraits just tumbled out of him. He had no notes and spoke spontaneously with charm and lilt."[31] Harry Blamires, one of his former students, says that Lewis was the biggest "draw" as a lecturer in the English school when he was a student there in the 1930's .

It was at an Oxford faculty meeting that Lewis first met Tolkien, who remained one of his closest friends until Lewis moved to Cambridge in 1954. Two other individuals who influenced his early intellectual and religious progress were Owen Barfield and Charles Williams. Barfield was a solicitor and amateur literary critic/philologist whom Lewis had met while an Oxford undergraduate. Charles Williams, the author of several idiosyncratic works of fiction and theology, was a man Lewis much admired and became acquainted with after sending Williams a letter praising his work. Lewis, Williams, and Tolkien met together on a semi-regular basis for many years to read and critique each others work. They were joined on occasion by Barfield and other friends and became known as the "Inklings."

# "THE UNHOLY MUDDLE"

*M*any can tell stories of powerful, convulsive moments and experiences which led to a dramatic conversion. Lewis is not one of these. His conversion came slowly over time and in several stages. As Warren wrote, his conversion "was no sudden plunge into a new life but rather a slow steady convalescence from a deep-seated spiritual illness of long standing."[32]

Lewis' childhood experiences of religion did nothing to encourage him to a life of faith. From an early age he was put off by the empty formalism of his family faith, and thus, before adulthood, he had rejected Christianity. But Lewis was a man too perceptive of spiritual realities to remain an atheist for very long. His reading of the literature of medieval England confirmed in him the important role that Christianity had played in shaping the culture he loved so much. Equally troubling to the security of his atheistic beliefs was the realization that many of his favorite authors, those whose view of the world was the most beautiful and sensible, had been profoundly influenced by the Christian worldview.

Perhaps the earliest major influence on Jack's thinking

about religion and truth was Owen Barfield, who convinced him of the error of Kirkpatrick's philosophical realism. The rationalistic Kirkpatrick had been a disciple of scientific materialism, the belief that the only reality is that which we can apprehend by our senses. This doctrine, Barfield pointed out, was at odds with Lewis' own experiences of romantic longing – experiences that suggested a reality beyond the purely physical. Materialism, he asserted, really failed to encompass reality. It could not explain the greatest mysteries of life, especially the mystery of the mind, and where thought originates. To say thinking is simply the result of chemical interactions in the brain was not a satisfying answer.

> *If one kept (as rock–bottom reality) the universe of the senses, aided by instruments and co–ordinated so as to form "science," then one would have to go much further…and adopt a Behaviouristic theory of logic, ethics and aesthetics. But such a theory was…unbelievable to me…I was therefore compelled to give up realism…Unless I were to accept an unbelievable alternative, I must admit that the mind was no late–come phenomenon; that the whole universe was, in the last resort, mental; that our logic was a participation in a cosmic Logos.*[33]

Reflection revealed to Jack that he was very drawn to the writings of Christians throughout the ages. If he thought they were wrong about God, he believed them to be right about almost everything else. He found G. K. Chesterton's *The Everlasting Man*, especially challenging, as it mapped out a Christian understanding of history that really made sense to

Lewis. An entry in his diary for January 18, 1927 reveals the spiritual confusion into which he was thrust by his growing suspicion that there was something more beyond the natural realm:

> *Imagination and Intellect and the Unholy*
> *Muddle I am in about them at present;*
> *undigested scraps of Anthroposophy and*
> *psychoanalysis jostling with orthodox idealism*
> *over a background of some good old Kirkian*
> *rationalism. Lord, what a mess! And all the*
> *time (with me) there's the danger of falling back*
> *into most childish superstitions, or of running*
> *into dogmatic materialism to escape them.*[34]

The conclusion of the first stage of Lewis' journey was a shift from naturalism to Theism. He was traveling up Headington Hill on the top floor of a bus when it came to him that he would have to make a decision about God. He could no longer ignore what he had begun to see as the truth and needed to make a choice. Through many intense conversations, the influence of his Christian friends led him to see the path he must choose. During the summer of 1929 he knelt in his rooms at Magdalen and "gave in, and admitted that God was God, and knelt and prayed; perhaps that night, the most dejected and reluctant convert in all England."[35] He had left behind the smug atheism of earlier years, but still did not yet embrace a fully orthodox view of God. Trying to understand how Jesus Christ fit into the picture was the most difficult issue for Lewis to resolve. He could not accept the Gospel records about who Jesus was.

A seemingly minor off-the-cuff remark by a respected, cynical professor named T. D. Weldon, haunted Lewis for months. Weldon was known for being a hardheaded skeptic who would only believe on the basis of concrete evidence. He was talking with Jack about some of the odd events of history when he remarked that the evidence for the veracity of the Gospels was quite strong. "Rum thing, that stuff of Fraser's about the Dying God," Weldon remarked, "It almost looks as if it really happened once."[36] Surprised, Lewis tried to get him to explain, but Weldon simply changed the subject. That Weldon would admit to the historical strength of the Christian message caused Lewis much discomfort, especially when his own investigation of the issues only confirmed Weldon's statement.

The determining issue that moved Lewis from Theism to Christianity was his developing understanding of the meaning of myth. A conversation with Tolkien and another friend, Hugo Dyson, finally helped him to arrive at a new conception of myth and how it relates to truth. Both of these men were Christians who had often argued these issues with Lewis. One evening, in an animated discussion, Lewis began to become convinced of the truth of their arguments.

> *Tolkien reiterated the argument already made*
> *familiar to Lewis by Barfield. We speak of 'stars'*
> *and 'trees' as though they were entities which*
> *we had mastered in our post-Newtonian, mate-*
> *rialist fashion. But for those who formed the*
> *words star and tree they were very different. For*
> *them, stars were living silver, bursting into*
> *flame in answer to an eternal music in the*
> *mind of God. All creation was "myth-woven*
> *and elf-patterned.*[37]

Lewis was still troubled by the idea that an action in the distant past could have real consequences for contemporary belief. The idea that Christ had somehow sacrificed Himself seemed patently absurd. How could His death possibly have saved the world? Tolkien's answer was that the earlier pagan myths were God's expression of Himself in the mind of the poets. Fragments of eternal truth were transmitted in a limited way as hints of God's plan. The old, recurring myth of the dying God had become an historical reality in the person of Christ. Myth had become fact, but it still retained the imagistic quality of a myth. It was not so important to fully comprehend the doctrine of the atonement as it was to live the reality of it as it had been provided in the death and resurrection of Christ. After Tolkien left that evening, Lewis wandered the streets of Oxford with Dyson, considering Tolkien's argument and talking of the implications of Christian faith. Twelve days later, following the motorcycle trip to the Whipsnade Zoo, Lewis wrote to Greeves that he had become a Christian.

# THE REGRESS OF AN OXFORD PILGRIM

*A*s soon as they saw the house, Jack and Mrs. Moore, along with Warren who had returned from the service, knew that this was just the sort of place they had been looking for. Called "the Kilns" because it was surrounded by kilns once used to fire bricks, this house in Headington Quarry was only about three miles from the center of Oxford, yet had the secluded feel that Jack so wanted. It was a lovely piece of property, half covered with trees and a pond and an old red-brick house that lay at the end of a driveway full of potholes. Here, in this peaceful setting, Lewis would spend the rest of his life.

Jack grew quickly in the faith that he had embraced. One of the first fruits of Lewis' conversion to Christianity was the book he published in 1933 called *The Pilgrim's Regress: An Allegorical Apology for Christianity, Reason and Romanticism.* Written during a two week stint in 1932 while vacationing in Ireland, it is an argument for the three things Lewis was always to hold most dear: orthodox Christianity, classical reason, and Lewis' own idiosyncratic version of Romanticism.

At the time he began work on this fictional piece, Lewis was already engaged in research for the book that would make his reputation as a literary scholar, *The Allegory of Love*. He determined to put to use the form of the allegory in *The Pilgrim's Regress*, which is modeled upon both John Bunyan's famous book and Langland's *Piers Plowman*. The book is a semi-autobiographical account of Lewis' own philosophical journey, using an "everyman" character named John, who follows the romantic longing of his heart, but finds that none of life's sensual distractions or philosophical abstractions will fulfill his quest. Only in the arms of Mother Kirk (the church) does he learn the real nature of his longing.

What brings John a clue to the meaning of life is his vision of a beautiful island and an inner voice which implores him to "Come." The vision leads him, throughout the book, to search for this island. The search for the satisfaction of this desire provides the motivation for John's journey, a pictorial account of Lewis' search for the meaning behind his own "Romantic" longings. As he explains in the preface to the second edition of the book:

> *What I meant was a particular recurrent experience which dominated my childhood and adolescence and which I hastily called "Romantic" because inanimate nature and marvelous literature were among the things that evoked it…The experience is one of intense longing. It is distinguished from other longings by two things. In the first place, though the sense of want is acute and even painful, yet the mere wanting is felt to be somehow a delight. This hunger is better than any other fullness; this poverty better than all other wealth…. In the second place, there is a peculiar mystery about the object of this Desire…It*

*appeared to me…that if a man diligently fol-*
*lowed this desire, pursuing the false objects*
*until their falsity appeared and then resolutely*
*abandoning them, he must come at last into*
*the clear knowledge that the human soul was*
*made to enjoy some object that is never fully*
*given—nay, cannot even be imagined as*
*given—in our present mode of subjective*
*and spatio–temporal existence.*[38]

This quote gives us an insight into the really important
themes of both the book and Lewis' life. Arguing for a particular kind of traditional frame of mind that combines and
balances intellectual and romantic concerns, in *Pilgrim's
Regress* he lashes out at those tendencies of modern thought
that would cause us to lose this balance.

Though it has never been considered among the best of
Lewis' books, *Pilgrim's Regress* has much to recommend it. In
it, Lewis raises many important issues and deals with them in
a way that is both wonderfully witty and penetratingly
insightful. Still, at times, the artfulness of the book is overshadowed by its didactic intents. Lewis himself writes in the
preface that "when allegory is at its best, it approaches myth,
which must be grasped with the imagination, not with the
intellect."[39] Unfortunately, *Pilgrim's Regress* generally fails to
reach this level as Lewis appeals much more to the intellect
than to the imagination, and relies on long passages of philosophical explanation to do what should be achievable by his
creative skills. As Lewis matured as a writer, he became more
able to explicate his themes by the use of powerful images
rather than dialectical arguments. One cannot help but wonder if Lewis himself saw the imperfections of this work, for
his next attempts at Christian writing were given to more

straightforward apologetics. When he later returned to fiction, it is obvious that he had learned something important about the writing of this genre.

The 1940's were a fertile time for C. S. Lewis. In addition to producing twelve books, he wrote a number of literary and religious essays, reviews, and some prefaces to the books of others. What marks his output at this time is a growing dependence upon reason (one of the triad he had defended in *Pilgrim's Regress*) as a key to defending the Christian faith. His work during this period shows a growing conviction that a reasonable and compelling case could be made for Christianity. His great trilogy of apologetic works, *The Problem of Pain*, *Mere Christianity*, and *Miracles*, shows a trust in the ability of reasoned argument to demonstrate the truth of the gospel.

In *The Problem of Pain*, for example, Lewis tackles the difficult problem of theodicy: the existence of evil and suffering in the light of an omnipotent God. His tone throughout the book is careful, not suggesting that he has done more with his argument than to provide some reasonable answers to difficult questions. His argument is clear and the writing, especially in the later chapters, is quite beautiful. Still, some of his academic colleagues were outraged that he would speak out about issues in which he had no academic training. This seemed to them unprofessional. The scholar should not write for the masses, as this will cause him to compromise his academic thoroughness. When Lewis took on the problem of evil, some thought he had bitten off more than he could chew. One colleague is reported to have said that the problem of pain was bad enough without Lewis making it worse!

It is indisputable that Lewis damaged his reputation among his colleagues by writing popular books that defended the Christian faith. Many Lewis scholars have conjectured that it was his colleagues' jealousy and irritation that kept him from ever receiving the academic honors and position his fine work in literary criticism obviously deserved. No one questioned his unique skills and breadth of knowledge, but some were annoyed that these gifts were imparted to the common man in the hope of converting them. To express such strong Christian ideals was considered by many colleagues to be intolerable and inappropriate in the rarefied air of Oxford.

# A VOICE FOR THE TRUTH

Jack shifted in his chair and adjusted his manuscript into an orderly pile, rehearsing again in his mind how he would speak his first sentences. He knew how important the first few lines were in grasping and holding the attention of his listeners. Today's audience, whom he was to address via radio, was the largest he had ever been privileged to speak to. How different it was to sit, almost alone in a studio crammed with electronic equipment, and speak into a microphone instead of lecturing a roomful of university students on the intricacies of Milton or medieval allegory. He raised a glass of water and quenched his dry throat. Here was an opportunity to express his convictions clearly and simply to a mass audience who suffered from the uncertainties and questionings brought on by the Second World War.

Dr. James Welch, director of religious broadcasting for the British Broadcasting Corporation, had been helped immensely by reading *The Problem of Pain*, and had approached Lewis with the idea of producing a series of lectures to be broadcast over the radio. Never very enthusiastic about modern technology, Jack was at first reticent. But he came to see that through this medium he could reach an audience that he would never reach through his books. Believing that one of the key problems of the modern age was the lack of conviction about absolute values, he proposed a series of lectures on the objective basis for right and wrong. Without the recovery of a sense of guilt, Lewis believed that there was little hope for the moral improvement of modern Britain.

Jack gave four live fifteen minute broadcasts during August 1941 billed as "Right and Wrong: A Clue to the Meaning of the Universe?" They were an immediate success. His rich voice, earthy but educated in its tones, communicated the same kind of enthusiasm for his subject that made him a popular University lecturer. He was sagely wise, but framed his arguments to be understood by the man on the street, spicing his talks with witty observations and self-deprecation. George Sayer remembers being in a pub filled with soldiers one evening when Jack began one of the broadcasts. "At a quarter to eight, the bartender turned the radio up for Lewis. 'You listen to this bloke,' he shouted. 'He's really worth listening to.' And those soldiers did listen attentively for the entire fifteen minutes."[40]

Lewis immediately began to receive letters from those who were helped or challenged by the radio broadcasts. He agreed to a further broadcast to answer some of the questions that correspondents had raised, and this led to more letters and further broadcasts. His next series of talks, entitled, "What Christians Believe," were an overview of the basic theology of the Christian faith. Once again, he handled his assignment with aplomb, avoiding controversy by focusing on the essential truths held by all believers and by avoiding denominational squabbles.

What impressed many listeners was the rationality and logic with which Lewis defended Christian beliefs. Many non-believers were accustomed to hearing more emotion-centered appeals and fiery rhetoric from Christian orators. Lewis' presentation stressed a reasonable and common sense appeal, put forward with dignity, respect and good humor. He emphasized the positive Christian virtues and was practical about how these might be lived out in the course of one's life.

Off and on throughout the war years, Lewis agreed to do other series of talks on such topics as "Christian Behaviour" and "Beyond Personality: The Christian View of God." Eventually these lectures were gathered together and published in book form under the now-familiar title, *Mere Christianity*. This book has remained one of Lewis' most popular non-fiction titles, still a bestseller almost fifty years later. His clarity, charity and charm have influenced scores of Christians, by presenting the Christian faith in a way both reasonable and attractive to the modern man. As Anthony Burgess has suggested, he is "the ideal persuader for the half-convinced, for the good man who would like to be a Christian but finds his intellect getting in the way."[41]

In addition to these lectures, and a similar series given on RAF bases, Lewis was instrumental in founding the Oxford Socratic Club, a debating society which pitted Christians and atheists against each other in honest intellectual debate on questions of importance. Over the years, these debates attracted some of the most well-known names in British intellectual circles, including Iris Murdoch, Konrad Lorenz, Charles Williams, Dorothy L. Sayers, J. Bronowski and J. B. S. Haldane. Lewis demonstrated that Christianity could hold its own in the intellectual sphere, and need not be purely defensive in its stance. More often than not, Lewis took the offensive. As one former member states: "If I have an adult Christian faith that is a rational one, I owe it to the meetings of the Socratic society. I never realized before I went there that Christianity could be defended logically, and that most of the arguments used by its opponents could be shown to be irrational."[42]

Through his radio talks, books, and public appearances Lewis had become, in a short span of time, one of the most visible public defenders of the faith.

# TOUR OF DUTY

WW II was a busy time for the Lewis household. The tumults of war did much to disrupt Jack's quiet life as an Oxford don. The government announced that those between the ages of eighteen and forty-one could be called up for service, and since Jack was only forty, he prepared himself for enlistment. Due to the massive conscriptions, it seemed unlikely that there would be any students left to teach. When he learned that there would indeed be undergraduates left at Oxford and that his position at the University exempted him from active duty, Lewis wanted to find a way to serve his country. He was very uncomfortable with the idea of doing nothing for the war effort while others fought and died.

When his offer to be an instructor of cadets was declined, he decided not to volunteer for duty with the Ministry of Information as it would involve the telling of lies as part of the propaganda campaign. Since these avenues of service were not possible for him, he joined the Oxford City Home Guard Battalion, a group of part-time soldiers whose job was to repel German troops who might attempt a landing by air.

Every Saturday morning he arose at half past one to perform his "tour of duty." Although he initially enjoyed the crisp night air and the stillness of Oxford at night, his interest soon wore off. He wrote to Arthur Greeves that he spent "one night in nine mooching about the most malodorous parts of Oxford with a rifle."[43] Despite his discomfort, however, he was glad to be doing his part.

His Home Guard work was not his only avenue of service. Jack and the Moores decided to open their home to children evacuated from London and other cities vulnerable to the vicious night-bombing by the Germans. The extra guests meant extra work in addition to his usual duties of sawing logs for the fire (coal was severely rationed) and hanging blackout curtains.

Jack immediately took a liking to the children who now filled his home. He had always been rather shy and awkward around children, not knowing how to relate to them very well, but now he had the opportunity to grow in affection and understanding of these youngsters. It is quite possible that without his experiences at this time, he would never have had the knowledge or desire to later write stories for children. The roots of the impulse to write the Narnia tales surely stem from this period of a house full of young ones.

One of Lewis' greatest worries during wartime concerned his brother Warren, who had been called back into service. Warren had developed a serious problem with alcohol, and stress only made his addiction worse. This battle with alcoholism, which is probably what led to Warren's discharge after only eleven months of service, continued throughout his life and was always a concern for Jack.

Although he was convinced of the justice of the war effort, Jack saw that it wasn't a simple matter of the good guys versus the bad guys. The increasingly anti-Christian forces that were destroying the West from within were paralleled by the Nazis who threatened it from without. "The sins of the democracies are very great. But very likely those of the total-itarian states are even greater."[44] Because of this, Lewis could not accept pacifism and recognized the need to meet evil on its own terms. His patriotism, however, was of a very open-eyed variety. Although he loved his country, he knew that his first allegiance was to the kingdom of heaven.

# SCREWTAPE

he idea for *The Screwtape Letters*, the book that helped to make Lewis a household word, came to him at church one morning in the autumn of 1942.

> *Before the service was over…I was struck by an*
> *idea for a book which I think would be both*
> *useful and entertaining. It would be called "As*
> *One Devil to Another" and would consist of let-*
> *ters from an elderly retired devil to a young*
> *devil who has just started work on his first*
> *"patient."…The idea would be to give all the*
> *psychology of temptation from the other point*
> *of view. . .*[45]

Once the idea was in his head, the writing came quickly. Each week he spent a couple of hours writing a letter until all thirty-one were completed. He sent them to *The Guardian,* a conservative newspaper, which published them one at a time over a period of months. The letters were an immediate success and were soon gathered together into a book. The first edition sold out before it came off the presses and was followed by eight more printings in the first year. This would become his most popular book, and it could have made him a moderately wealthy man. Ultimately, over two million copies would be sold, and it would be translated into sixteen different languages. But Lewis, never valuing riches very highly, consigned two thirds of all his royalties to a charitable trust, and much of the rest was soon given over to others in need.

The lasting appeal of *The Screwtape Letters* is surely its combination of wit (it is a very funny book!) and psychological perceptions into belief and disbelief, along with its wealth of spiritual insights about the practical living of the Christian life. In this collection of letters from Screwtape (an experienced devil who holds a high position in the Infernal Civil Service) to his nephew Wormwood (who is just learning the arts of temptation), Lewis reveals brilliant insights about prayer, humility, the meaning of pleasure, obedience, gluttony, greed, love, lust, marriage, and liberal theology. His grasp of the psychology of evil was so acute that not everyone caught the satire involved. Lewis delighted in telling of the country parson who wrote to the editor of *The Guardian* to cancel his subscription because "much of the advice given in these letters seemed to him not only to be erroneous but positively diabolical."[46]

Many times, in this work, Jack's satire is rapier sharp, particularly when dealing with liberal pseudo-Chrisitianity. Because he took evil seriously, he did not underestimate the ability of the devil to derail the lives of believers or to blind the eyes of the non-believer to the truth. But as always, his focus was more on the power of good, and God's provision to his children. Lewis never liked to concentrate his thought on the power of evil, when he could speak instead of the graciousness of God.

The years between 1942 and 1946 were productive ones for Lewis. In addition to *The Screwtape Letters*, he published some of his most famous books during these years: *A Preface to Paradise Lost, Beyond Personality, Perelandra, That Hideous Strength, The Great Divorce* and *The Abolition of Man.* The latter has to be considered one of his most important legacies for our time as he tackles the thorny issue of the objectivity of right and wrong. Right and wrong are realities, he argued, not merely subjective preferences for us to choose between. There is a Moral Law that is written into the heart and conscience of every man and woman and we ignore it at our peril. For its uncompromising and logical attack upon moral relativism, *The Abolition of Man* deserves consideration as one of the most important works of the twentieth century. If anything, it is more relevant today than when it was first written.

# The Inklings

The tea kettle's shrill whistle announced the near arrival of tea, which would be nice and strong; Warren always saw to that. Those who smoked lit up their pipes and settled themselves into chairs as their smoke drifted toward the ceiling.

"Well, has nobody got anything to read us?," Jack ventured. Of course, he usually had something he was working on at the ready, but this time Tolkien offered to read some more of what he called "the new Hobbit" (eventually published as *The Lord of the Rings*).

Such was the ritual for meetings of the Inklings. Readings from works in progress, criticism from other members, or perhaps an argument on philosophy or ethics. Sometimes, when no one had anything to share, the evening took on a more riotous aspect, full of laughter and verbal jousting. Talk at the Inklings gatherings was described by Warren as "an outpouring of wit, nonsense, whimsy, dialectical swordplay, and pungent judgments."[47] Their discussions ranged from literary criticism to thorny theological issues and speculation on such questions as whether dogs had souls.

When they did fall into discussion of each others work, this was no mutual admiration society. "Praise for good work was unstinted but censure for bad, or even not so good, was often brutally frank."[48] Tolkien, for example, so disliked *The Lion, the Witch and the Wardrobe*, that Lewis considered abandoning the project. Thankfully, another member came to its defense and encouraged him to continue writing!

The Inklings were never really a club or literary society, but simply a gathering of friends who shared a love for good books and good conversation. Over the yeaes, its members included: Jack and Warren, Tolkien, Charles Williams, Nevill Coghill, Hugo Dyson, Owen Barfield, Adam Fox, Dr. 'Humphrey' Havard, Gervase Mathew, Colin Hardie, Christopher Tolkien and John Wain. They met in Jack's rooms at Magdalen every Thursday evening after dinner. During the war years they often shared a cold meal, part of the bounty that was mailed to Lewis from American admirers who knew that food could be scarce during the rationing in Britain. Another ritual among the Inklings was to meet before lunch on Tuesdays at a local pub called The Eagle and Child. It was christened by the group as "The Bird and Baby" and has also entered into the lore of the Inklings.

In a letter to Warren, Jack vividly captures what made the meetings of the Inklings so extraordinary:

> *On Thursday we had a meeting of the Inklings*
> *– you and Coghill both absented unfortunately.*
> *We dined at the Eastgate. I have never in my*
> *life seen Dyson so exuberant—"a roaring*
> *cataract of nonsense." The bill of fare after-*
> *wards consisted of a section of the new Hobbit*
> *book from Tolkien, a nativity play from*
> *Williams (unusually intelligible for him, and*

*approved by all) and a chapter out of the book on the Problem of Pain from me. It so happened—it would take too long to explain why—that the subject matter of the three readings formed almost a logical sequence, and produced a really first rate evening's talk of the usual wide-ranging kind—"from grave to gay, from lively to severe." I wished very much we could have had you with us.*[49]

One of the greatest delights of the Inklings was the companionship of Charles Williams, whom Lewis had first come to know when he wrote Williams an enthusiastic letter to commend him on his fascinating novel, *The Place of the Lion.* On meeting him, Lewis took an immediate liking to this unusual and very gifted amateur scholar. Drawn by the sense of goodness which radiated from him and by his vivid imaginative powers, Lewis soon came under his spell and encouraged friends to read Williams' works.

Williams moved to Oxford from London in 1939 and at once became a core member of the Inklings. Jack arranged for him to give lectures at the University and found publishers for some of his work. He also wrote a commentary on one of Williams' Arthurian poem cycles and even tried to get him a professorship of poetry, even though Williams had never earned a University degree.

What drew people to Williams was his presence and his power of speech. As Lewis described him, "In appearance he was tall, slim, and straight as a boy, though grey-haired. His face we thought ugly: I am not sure that the word 'monkey' has not been murmured in this context. But the moment he spoke it became, as was also said, like the face of an angel—not a feminine angel in the debased tradition of some religious art, but a masculine angel, a spirit burning with intelligence and clarity."[50]

Williams once gave a lecture on Milton's *Comus* which surprised Lewis because of its effect on its undergraduate listeners. It was, as Lewis remembered it, not so much a study of *Comus* as a lecture on the virtue of chastity. Lewis found it superb as literary criticism, but even more memorable as a "sermon" on chastity. As he recounts it in a letter to Warren:

> *It was a beautiful sight to see a whole room*
> *full of modern young men and women sitting*
> *in that absolute silence which can not be*
> *faked, very puzzled, but spell-bound: perhaps*
> *with something of the same feeling which a lec-*
> *ture on unchastity might have evoked in their*
> *grandparents—the forbidden subject broached*
> *at last. He forced them to lap it up and I think*
> *many, by the end, liked the taste more than*
> *they expected to. It was "borne in upon me"*
> *that that beautiful carved room had probably*
> *not witnessed anything so important since the*
> *great medieval or Reformation lectures. I have*
> *at last, if only for once, seen a University doing*
> *what it was founded to do: teaching Wisdom.*[51]

When Lewis told fellow Inkling Hugo Dyson about this lecture, Dyson quipped, "the fellow's becoming a common *chastitute*."[52]

Lewis probably loved Williams above any of his friends. They shared a vision of Christianity and Romanticism, fired by a love of both orthodoxy and vivid speculation. Jack always thought that Charles Williams was the very personification of human goodness. When Charles died suddenly in May of

1945, it was a loss of the deepest kind Williams' passing, however, strengthened Jack's faith, changing the way that he thought about death. "It has made," he wrote, "the next world much more real and palpable."[53] In a group of essays by Lewis and other Inklings members entitled *Essays Presented to Charles Williams*, Lewis recalls his friend.

> *No event has so corroborated my faith in the next world as Williams did simply by dying. When the idea of death and the idea of Williams thus met in my mind, it was the idea of death that was changed.*[54]

# THE HUMBLE APOLOGIST

*J*ack settled back heavily in his chair overcome by an uncommon feeling. He, the master debater, had been defeated at his own game. He had always loved to challenge the sloppy thinking of others. Now, really for the first time, he had been called to task and had been unable to adequately defend his argument. His contention was that naturalism (the belief in only what can be perceived by the senses) is self-refuting. He knew that his idea was fundamentally correct, but he had been bested in the debate by failing to account for the philosophical intricacies his opponent had raised.

The debate had its birth in the publication of his book, *Miracles*, which shows Lewis at the peak of apologetic confidence. A more dense and difficult book than his earlier volumes, *Miracles* argues that human reason requires a supernatural Reason, outside of itself, to lend it validity. Lewis attempts to secure the case for a supernatural realm by the use of close argumentation. As might be expected, the book is filled with rich insights, sharp wit, penetrating observation and argument from homely analogies. Some critics felt, however, that Lewis had pressed beyond what was actually provable by reason.

A turning point in Jack's career as an apologetic writer came in his debate with Oxford philosopher G.E.M. (Elizabeth) Anscombe. In a public debate held on February 2, 1948, Anscombe attacked Lewis for his criticism of naturalism in the third chapter of *Miracles*. Although Anscombe was herself a Christian, she felt that Lewis had tried to argue beyond what reason could actually posit. The attack was devastating. Dining two days later with Derek Brewer, Lewis recalled the debate with horror. "His imagery was all of the fog of war, the retreat of infantry thrown back under heavy attack."[55] Many of those present testified to Anscombe's clear victory in the intellectual combat. Lewis must have thought so too, for in the next edition of the book he made some major changes in the argument. At the time he was devastated and humbled by his defeat. "I can never write another book of that sort," he once said to George Sayer, referring to *Miracles*.[56]

After this debate Lewis turned his attentions more to the intuitive argument of a well-told story and to what common human experiences and the Scriptures reveal to us, placing less emphasis on the overtly apologetic work that made up such a large part of his earlier writings. When he did speak of the apologetic task, he was more circumspect and spoke of the limitations of a purely rational defense of belief. "Christians and their opponents," he wrote, "again and again expect that some new discovery will either turn matters of faith into matters of knowledge or else reduce them to patent absurdities. But this has never happened."[57] And he wrote to Dorothy L. Sayers, herself a novelist and apologist of some distinction, "Apologetic work is so dangerous to one's own faith. A doctrine never seems dimmer to me than when I have just successfully defended it."[58] Perhaps he captures this attitude best in a poem entitled "The Apologist's Evening Prayer":

*From all my lame defeats and oh! much more*
*From all my victories that I seemed to score;*
*From cleverness shot forth on Thy behalf*
*At which while angels weep, the audience laugh;*
*From all my proofs of Thy divinity,*
*Thou who wouldst give no sign, deliver me. . .*
*Lord of the narrow gate and the needle's eye,*
*Take from me all my trumpery lest I die.*[59]

Lewis came to see that just as reason is the organ of truth, imagination is the organ of meaning. It was only the imagination that could reveal the depths of reality, moving beyond the abstractions and arguments which so entangle us. He realized that, as his friend Tolkien had argued, abstract arguments for doctrines were really less true than myths, for reality is too all-encompassing for the finite mind to fully comprehend. Stories take us beyond ideas into the very experience of truth. After all, it was the promise of fulfilling the longing awakened by myths that had brought about Lewis' own conversion, rather than careful logical analysis. Although he never ceased to believe in the power of the intellect to grasp truth, it was in stories, Lewis found, that the truth of the Christian gospel could best be embodied and communicated.

# EUCHATASTROPHE

*J*. R. R. Tolkien coined the phrase "euchatastrophe" as a way to distinguish the Christian story from other mythic traditions. A "euchatastrophe," he wrote, is "the good catastrophe, the sudden joyous 'turn'…it denies universal final defeat and in so far is evangelium, giving a fleeting glimpse of Joy, Joy beyond the walls of the world, poignant as grief."[60]

The Christian gospel is the ultimate euchatastrophe, the ultimate tale of the triumph of goodness. It was this tale that Lewis sought to tell in his powerful fiction works. They not only reflect the Christian tradition, but do so in such a way that they draw on the mythic strength, the fairy-tale quality of the gospel story.

Lewis had been using his creativity in the service of the truth from the publication of his very first post-conversion book. But it was with his "Space Trilogy" that this quality came to full fruition. In his trilogy of books *Out of the Silent Planet*, *Perelandra*, and *That Hideous Strength*, Lewis presented many of the classic themes of Christian doctrine in a new and imaginative way. The books have the virtue of being genuinely pleasurable to read, avoiding the weight of too much didactic exposition. He doesn't merely tell us the story, he shows us and helps us to feel its power. He "*remythologizes*" the gospel story by recasting it in a different and unexpected framework.

There are several qualities that make this series highly successful as an attempt at remythologization. Foremost among them is that Lewis has created a world believable in its own right, and yet has illustrated Christian themes in that world in such a way that they seem fresh and unexpected to those reared in the "Christianized" Western culture. They have a reality all their own. Lewis did not simply tack on the Christian tradition, but actually imagined how it might apply in an entirely different context. He did this so successfully that many critics failed to recognize the presence of any Christian theology in the novels. In a letter written after the publication of the first volume of the trilogy, Lewis expressed his surprise that this was the case:

> *You will be both grieved and amused to hear that out of about 60 reviews only two showed any knowledge that my idea of the fall of the Bent One was anything but an invention of my own...any amount of theology can now be smuggled into people's minds under the cover of romance without their knowing it.*[61]

Lewis' first intention, however, was not to proselytize, but rather to create a new mythic representation of the truth as he perceived it and to tell a good story with a serious intent. "My *Out of the Silent Planet*...is a critique of our own age only as any Christian work is implicitly a critique of any age. I was trying to redeem for genuinely serious purposes the form popularly known in this country as science fiction."[62]

One of the strongest qualities in these books, which causes them to lodge in your brain long after you close the covers of the book, is the strength of Lewis' descriptive passages, which powerfully evoke the strangeness of the planets involved in the story. There are passages which create a strong sense of the numinous, an awe-fulness and other-ness in the presence of a mysterious Other. Of course that Other is a picture of God and the supernatural realm. The message of the three volumes taken together points to the inherent order of both the cosmos and human society under the control of the Creator, and exposes the chaos and evil that result when human beings attempt to control their own destinies apart from God.

Lewis' other great mythic work for adults is *Till We Have Faces*, which he felt was his greatest fictional achievement. More than in any other work, he allowed the imaginative element to take precedence over the rational. Hence, this is a somewhat more difficult work, with many layers of meaning. The book does not have the straightforward thrust of narrative that we have come to expect from Lewis, but it more than makes up for this by the richness of its characterization and the complexity of its themes.

The story can be read as an allegory of the soul's journey toward God, and the necessity of stripping away the false illusions of the self in order to know and be known. As Orual, the main character, says:

> *When the time comes to you at which you will be forced to utter the speech which has lain at the centre of your soul for years, which you have, all that time, idiot-like, been saying over and over, you'll not talk about joy of words. I saw well why the Gods do not speak to us openly, nor let us answer. Till that word can be*

*dug out of us, why should they hear the babble
that we think we mean? How can they meet us
face to face until we have faces?*[63]

By remythologizing the Christian story, Lewis attempted
to awaken a longing for God by providing fresh images of the
divine: The Landlord (*Pilgrim's Regress*), Maledil the Old (*The
Space Trilogy*), the God of the Mountain (*Till We Have Faces*),
and possibly the most powerful, Aslan (*The Chronicles of
Narnia*). Both the heart and the spirit are captured by these
stories and thus become the pioneers, blazing a trail which
the mind can later follow with reason and cogitation.

# Narnia

*I* am glad you liked The Lion," Lewis wrote in response to a letter from an appreciative reader. "A number of mothers, and still more, schoolmistresses, have decided that it is likely to frighten children, so it is not selling very well. But the real children like it, and I am astonished how some very young ones seem to understand it. I think it frightens some adults, but very few children."64

Probably what causes some adults to be frightened by the Narnian tales is that they deal with the most pressing of ultimate issues: the reality of evil, the ultimate power of good, the nature of faith, and the hope of the Christian life. Though they never stoop to the level of propaganda, the message of the gospel is clearly found in their pages. Of course the comments of concern over slow sales were obviously ill-founded, for these stories have taken their justifiably high place as classic children's books and now sell hundreds of thousands of copies a year.

In *The Chronicles of Narnia* we perhaps get our best glimpse of Lewis' personal faith. A. N. Wilson suggests that "Narnia *is* the inside of Lewis' mind, peopled with a rich enjoyment of old books and old stories and the beauties of nature."[65] We also see his love for God, his desire for holiness, and the recognition of his own sinful nature. We are able to participate in his childlike wonder in God's mercy as Lewis makes the "old, old story" seem so fresh and new. Lewis addresses the child in the adult and the adult in the child.

One of the great joys of Narnia is that it is never heavy-handed. We don't get bogged down while Lewis tries to teach us something. He lets the innate power of the story operate in our hearts to make the message real. Although all the key elements of Christian theology are here (creation, temptation, the fall, death, judgment, redemption, heaven) he did not want his readers to feel that they were reading a work of veiled theology. Instead, he saw the goal of the Narnian tales as that of preparing his reader for the gospel. As biographer and long-time friend George Sayer has written,

> *His idea, as he once explained it to me, was to make it easier for children to accept Christianity when they met it later in life. He hoped that they would be vaguely reminded of the somewhat similar stories that they had read and enjoyed years before. "I am aiming at a sort of pre-baptism of the child's imagination."*[66]

Once again, as with the other mythic fiction, Lewis longed to awaken the reader's longing for God. Lewis' former pupil and long-time friend Dom Bede Griffiths says,

> *The figure of Aslan tells us more about how Lewis understood the nature of God than anything else he wrote. It has all His hidden power and majesty and awesomeness which Lewis*

*associated with God, but also His glory and*
*tenderness and even the humor which He*
*believed belonged to Him, so that children*
*could run up to Him and throw their arms*
*around Him and kiss Him.*[67]

The letters he received showed just how successful he
had been in the attempt to demonstrate God's character. To
one mother who wrote that she was concerned because her
son was more interested in Aslan than in Jesus, Lewis wrote:

*Laurence can't really love Aslan more than*
*Jesus, even if he feels that's what he is doing.*
*For the things he loves Aslan for doing or say-*
*ing are simply the things Jesus really did and*
*said. So that when Laurence thinks he is loving*
*Aslan, he is really loving Jesus: and perhaps*
*loving Him more than he ever did before.*[68]

# MENTOR BY LETTER

*J*ack sighed aloud as he looked over the stack of mail the postman had delivered. More letters, requiring more replies, to be added to a stack still waiting to be answered. With all the pressures of tutorials, lectures to write, student essays to read, research to be done, and galleys to correct for his next book, it seemed a daunting task to set to work on answering the letters that had come to him from all over the world. His fame had been unsought, but the people who had been touched by his books reached out to him as a long-distance spiritual mentor.

Some of the letters were of the congratulatory "fan mail" sort, but an increasing number sought Lewis' advice on spiritual matters or perplexing theological questions. More than one shared deep struggles and personal problems. The letter which lay before him was from a woman whose husband had taken a mistress. She was unsure how a Christian should respond to him or the situation. Jack took his pen in hand to answer her, crafting a letter that was both sympathetic and practical in tone while at the same time weighing the demands of the gospel.

At times, all the letter writing he had to do seemed over-whelming. In a letter to Vera Gebbert he writes:

> *The ghastly daily grind of unavoidable letters*
> *leaves me very ill disposed to pleasanter and*
> *friendlier correspondence. It is now 9:50 am*
> *and I've already been writing letters as hard as*
> *I can drive the pen across the paper for an hour*
> *and a half: and when on earth I shall get a*
> *chance to begin my own work I don't know...*[69]

It would have been easy to justify ignoring all the piles of correspondence as a distraction to his true calling, but Lewis saw the burdensome job of responding to the letters as a part of the vocation to which God had called him. He took the time to answer each one personally, not dismissing any of them. If a letter did not require a personal response, Warren often assisted by penning a reply. The letters poured in from former students, eager readers of his books, American college profes-sors and students, priests (one of whom he corresponded with in Latin!), housewives, and even children. In fact, there is a whole volume of letters which contains his correspondence to children.[70] With them, as with everyone else, he was never con-descending, but treated their thoughts and ideas seriously.

Because of the well thought out responses he made to the inquiries of his readers, Lewis' letters still make valuable, interesting and instructive reading today. All of his best qual-ities as a writer come to the fore in the published collections of his letters. Here, too, we see the heart of Lewis revealed, his kindness as an attentive listener to people's questions and struggles, his gentleness in critiquing the amateurish poems sent by an admirer and would-be poetess, his vivid humor and description of his domestic life. Although Lewis saw answering these letters as a very personal ministry, they have survived to continue a public sharing of his gifts.

# CAMBRIDGE

*A*ll the correspondence that Jack faced was made even more overwhelming by the increased load of domestic duties which he had to bear. The combination of varicose veins, which caused her a great deal of pain, and a lingering illness had made Janie Moore unable to do much around the house. As her illness progressed, her temper shortened and she found it hard to keep maids. Most of them only lasted a short time before they tired of her outbursts and her unreasonable demands. This left a large part of the burden directly on Jack. As he wrote in a letter:

> *For most men, Saturday afternoon is a free*
> *time, but I have an invalid lady to look after*
> *and the weekend is the time when I have no*
> *freedom at all, and have to try to be Nurse,*
> *Kennel-Maid, Wood-cutter, Butler,*
> *House-maid and Secretary all in one.*[71]

The years after the war were made difficult by both Janie's illness and Warren's increasing problem with alcoholism. He was in and out of treatment and recovery facilities and had become a real source of worry to Jack. Somehow Lewis was never able to muster a "tough love" sentiment toward Warren and allowed himself to be put upon without much complaint. He was silent about his struggles to all but his very closest friends.

In the spring of 1950, at a doctor's insistence, Janie had to be moved out of the Kilns and into a nursing home. Jack visited her nearly every day, although she had become so senile as to be verbally abusive and childishly petulant. He put up with her tantrums and the times she broke down into helpless tears because he felt a sense of duty toward her. He was convinced that his visits helped to ease her misery. She died of influenza in January of 1951.

Janie's death was something of a liberation for Jack. He suddenly found himself with more freedom and more control of his own time. His own health, which had not been very good over the previous few years, improved greatly and he looked forward to new academic achievements, only to be turned down again for academic promotion by colleagues who resented his growing popularity with the public.

He finally brought to conclusion a long term project he had been commissioned to write, a volume of the prestigious series *The Oxford History of English Literature*. His contribution was to be a study of the sixteenth century, a project which demanded a great deal of reading, even for one as well-read as Lewis. He found much of the writing of this period to be tiresome, clumsy in style and monotonous. "All the authors write like elderly men,"[72] he opined in the opening page. But unwilling to offer an opinion on a book he had not actually read, he labored on. Lewis was a man who loved to reread books that he had enjoyed, but more than once during this project as he scribbled the date he finished reading on the final page, he followed it with the phrase "never again."

The book, begun in 1944, was not published until 1954. It was immediately recognized as a brilliant work of literary history, a tour de force. Added to its authoritative completeness and intellectual vigor was the sly humor which made it enjoyable as well. Tolkien thought it was Lewis' finest book. It was followed in 1955 by *Surprised by Joy*, an autobiography that he had worked on sporadically for a number of years. Although incomplete as a biography, it is a delight for its insight into Lewis' inner life, his spiritual and intellectual journey to faith.

When some of his admirers at Cambridge heard that Jack had again been passed over for advancement and that he was frustrated with many of the educational innovations at Oxford, they proposed to the Cambridge English faculty that a new chair in Medieval and Renaissance studies be created especially for him. In 1954 he accepted this appointment, with some trepidation, for he hated change. He soon found that he was delighted with his new academic home. He lived in Oxford during the weekends and vacations and in Cambridge during the school week. He even came to love the train ride between the two for its leisurely pace and beautiful scenery. When he was invited to address the school in his inaugural lecture, he took the opportunity to deplore many of the trends of the modern world and to remind his listeners that they must always be attentive to the lessons of the past. This rather controversial stand was the talk of the University for weeks after.

One of the appeals of Cambridge was that it was not as entrenched in secularism. As Warren wrote in his diary, "Oxford…is the hardboiled materialistic scientific university. At Cambridge, the majority of dons and undergraduates are Christians."[73] If this was something of an exaggeration, it is probably still a reflection of the greater sense of acceptance that Lewis felt at Cambridge. "Cambridge is fun," Jack wrote, "such a country town feeling."[74]

# SURPRISED BY JOY

*F*or Jack, it was probably just a courtesy lunch with a frequent letter writer from the United States. For Joy, it was the chance to meet the man whose books had had such a powerful influence on her Christian growth. Having long been correspondents through the mail, Lewis finally met Joy Davidman Gresham at an Eastgate Hotel in Oxford.[75] He had been charmed by the quick wit and penetrating insights of her letters and was willing to meet with her when she visited from the United States. No one would have guessed, least of all Lewis the confirmed bachelor, that she would grow to be the great love of his life.

Joy Davidman was born in New York City, in 1915, to parents who were Jews from Eastern Europe. A precocious child and a great reader, she embraced the atheism of her father at an early age after reading H. G. Wells' *Outline of History*. Despite her early atheism, she had a poetic nature that she could never ignore. "She rejected all morality and saw nothing to live for except pleasure, and yet she had supernatural or mystical experiences rather like Jack's own."[76] She earned an M.A. in English literature from Columbia by the age of twenty and taught English in various New York high schools before joining the Communist party, where she became a tireless worker. She published a book of poetry entitled *Letter to a Comrade* which won the prestigious Yale Poetry Award for 1938 and followed this with a novel. She was also, for a time, the poetry editor and film critic for a Communist paper, then attempted a short-lived career as a Hollywood screen writer.

In 1942, Joy met William Gresham at a Communist party meeting and was immediately charmed by his style, intelligence and brash self-confidence. They soon married and had two children. Over time, both William and Joy gradually became disillusioned with Communism and left the party. When Bill's novel, *Nightmare Alley*, was made into a film, it brought sudden affluence to the Gresham household. But Bill found himself unable to deal with the pressures of his new-found fame and good fortune, spending money recklessly and reverting to an old nemesis, alcoholism.

One night he called from his office to tell Joy that he was going mad and did not know what to do. He could not come home, he said and then hung up. Joy found herself in desperation. She called back to the office, but he was not there, so she called everywhere she could think of in the hope of locating him. When he was nowhere to be found, she felt frightened, alone, and in real despair. It was a moment that changed her forever. As she later described it:

> *All my defenses—the walls of arrogance and cocksureness and self-love behind which I had hid from God—went down momentarily. And God came in.*[77]

She felt the reality of God's presence with her that night for the first time. God had come to her as a person, one so real that all doubts were dispelled. She found herself on her knees praying. When Bill eventually did come home, she told him of her experience and the two began studying theology together. Later, he prayed that God would rescue him from alcoholism, an addiction which had plagued him for many years, and they began to attend church together.

One of the earliest writers to influence Joy in her new-found faith was C. S. Lewis. She wrote to him for the first time in 1950. Both Jack and Warren found her letter amusing and well-written. More letters followed as she wrote for advice about her deteriorating marriage. Bill had become interested in Zen Buddhism and Scientology and had begun to use the I Ching to make decisions. He became increasingly abusive and began to be unfaithful to her.

When she finally arranged a trip to England to meet Lewis face to face, the meeting was a splendid success. Jack was charmed by her quick and logical mind, her blunt opinionated manner and her brilliant sense of humor. Many of his friends disliked her, finding her rude and opinionated, but Jack quickly developed a friendship with her. It was unusual for him to meet someone who was his equal as a conversationalist, but Joy could most definitely hold her own with him.

There were more meetings with Jack and Warnie during her time in England, visits to favorite pubs, readings of not yet published works and a lovely Christmas turkey prepared by Joy. Jack greatly enjoyed companionship, but began to become concerned that her idea of their relationship went beyond friendship. "Joy was no longer invited to stay at the Kilns; Lewis was even known to have hidden upstairs and pretended to be out when he saw her coming up the drive."[78]

Joy returned to the United States only to find that Bill was having an affair with her cousin and wanted a divorce. After some soul searching, she granted it and returned with the two boys, David and Douglas, to live in England. They took up residence in London and saw Jack only occasionally. During one visit, Jack showed the boys the typescript of *The Horse and His Boy* and let them know he planned to dedicate it to them. In 1955, Joy and her sons moved to Oxford, to a home only a mile or so from the Kilns and began to be frequent visitors at the Lewis home.

Just after he began to teach at Cambridge, Jack experienced a severe case of writer's block for the first time ever. He seemed to have run out of impetus. When he mentioned to Joy some ideas for a book he was contemplating, she set to work to help him refine his thoughts and became a valuable critic during the writing of the book. This book, entitled *Till We Have Faces* is considered by many critics to be his greatest fictional achievement, and it gives evidence of a growing emotional self-awareness within Jack. Much credit for the quality of the finished book must certainly be given to Joy, whose influence can be seen throughout.

# IN SICKNESS AND IN HEALTH

*I*n early 1960, when Joy's passport ran out, the only way she could stay in England was to marry an Englishman. She desperately wanted to remain in Britain and raise the boys there, so Jack decided that he would marry her in a civil ceremony. It would be a purely formal arrangement for the purpose of allowing her to maintain residence in England. The ceremony would not be performed in a church and would be kept a secret. There was no thought of them actually living together, for in Jack's mind it was a simple matter of charity to a dear friend. It was clear that at this time, as Sayer writes, that "he liked and admired her in a number of ways, but he was not in love with her, and this would not be a real marriage."[79]

Not long after the "marriage," Joy began to suffer severe pains in her legs, back, and chest. They became so severe that she had difficulty walking and in caring for the boys. After a fall that left her in great pain and unable to get up, she was taken to the hospital where an X-ray revealed the spread of cancer. Jack spent a great deal of time with her during the illness and found within himself the awakening of something beyond friendly affection. He wrote to one friend, "Never have I loved her more than since she was struck down."[80]

It soon became obvious that Joy was dying and Jack began to realize the great depth of his love for her. "It will," he wrote to Arthur Greeves, "be a great tragedy for me to lose her."[81] Lewis determined to really marry her; this time in a proper Christian ceremony.

On Christmas Eve of 1956, a notice appeared in the *London Times* that C. S. Lewis and Joy Gresham had been married in the Churchill Hospital in Oxford. In Jack's mind, he was marrying a dying woman. As Warren describes the ceremony in his diary:

> *At 11 a.m. we all gathered in Joy's room at the Wingfield—Bide [who performed the ceremony], J. [Jack], sister [the nurse], and myself, communicated, and the wedding was celebrated. I found it heartrending, and especially J's eagerness for the pitiable consolation of dying under the same roof as J: though to feel pity for anyone so magnificently brave as Joy is almost an insult. She is to be moved here next week and will sleep in the common room, with a resident hospital nurse installed in Vera's room. There seems to be little left to hope but that there may be no pain in the end.[82]*

# HAPPINESS AND JOY

But this was not the end. Jack and Joy were to enjoy just over three years of married life together.

Peter Bide, the Anglican priest who had performed the ceremony, had also laid hands on Joy and prayed for her healing. Jack, too, spent long hours in prayer, offering himself as a substitute, asking God to take some of her pain away and place it upon him. The results were miraculous. She had come home to the Kilns in April of 1957 to die, but by the end of the month she was up and moving about the house. Her remission had begun.

Jack on the other hand, seemed to have also had his prayers answered. By the middle of the summer he was in intense pain with a condition the doctors diagnosed as osteoporosis, the weakening of the bones caused by a reduction in their calcium content. "The intriguing thing," he wrote to a friend, "was that while I (for no discernible reason) was losing calcium from my bones, Joy, who needed it much more, was gaining it in hers."[83] But Jack's pain could not discourage him, for he was able to offer his own comfort for someone he had grown to care for deeply.

Both of them found their health much improved in 1958 and were able to make improvements around the house and take a long overdue trip to Ireland, his childhood home. The days of married life were filled with much happiness of a kind that had eluded Lewis for all his adult life. Once, while speaking to Coghill, he looked across the grassy quadrangle at Joy and said, "I never expected to have, in my sixties, the happiness that passed me by in my twenties."[84] Lewis was in love. And though they knew that her remission would not last forever, they treasured the time they had together.

In late 1959, a routine check-up at the hospital showed that the cancer had returned. "This last check," he wrote to Roger Lancelyn Green, "is the only one we approached without dread—her health seemed so complete. It is like being recaptured by the giant when you have passed every gate and are almost out of sight of his castle."[85] Can one have the presumption to ask for a second miracle? he asked himself.

A second miracle did not occur, but they made the most of the little time they had left. Her decline in health was gradual, so they carried on with their lives as though they had years left together. The highlight of Joy's last days was a trip to Greece, one of her lifelong dreams. It was a marvelous eleven days, filled with laughter and beauty. There was a slight improvement in her health in May and June, but on June 20 she was taken to the Acland nursing home when she could not stop vomiting.

She died on July 11. Her last two remarks to Lewis were: "You have made me very happy" and "I am at peace with God."

# A GRIEF OBSERVED

*J*ack's love for Joy had radically changed the life of this former bachelor, and her death left an immense gap in his life.

> *For those few years H. [Joy's first name was actually Helen] and I feasted on love; every mode of it—solemn and merry, romantic and realistic, sometimes as dramatic as a thunderstorm, sometimes as comfortable and unemphatic as putting on your soft slippers…The most precious gift that marriage gave me was this constant impact of something very close and intimate yet all the time unmistakably other, resilient—in a word, real…No cranny of heart or body remained unsatisfied.*[86]

He struggled to deal with her death and recorded his feelings in a book, *A Grief Observed.* This book is the sometimes painfully honest record of his struggles with doubt occasioned by Joy's passing and ultimately the conviction of faith which helped him to emerge from despair. Early in the book we read:

> …[W]here is God?…go to Him when your need is desperate, when all other help is vain, and what do you find? A door slammed in your face, and a sound of bolting and double bolting on the inside. After that, silence.[87]

Later in the book he writes,

> I have gradually been coming to feel that the door is no longer shut and bolted. Was it my own frantic need that slammed it in my face? The time when there is nothing at all in your soul except a cry for help may be just the time when God can't give it: you are like the drowning man who can't be helped because he clutches and grabs. Perhaps your own reiterated cries deafen you to the voice you hoped to hear.
>
> On the other hand, "Knock and it shall be opened." But does knocking mean hammering and kicking the door like a maniac?[88]

This kind of honesty is what gives the book its greatness and why it has helped so many who are struggling with the loss of a loved one. It was published under a pseudonym (N. W. Clerk) and released so that others could find help in their own struggles. Lewis was known to send it to people who had lost a loved one with the note that it was by a man he knew. The actual sales of the book were very modest until it was reissued under his own name, after his death.

In the months following Joy's death Lewis also worked on

*An Experiment in Criticism*, a delightful book about becoming a better reader, and *Letters to Malcolm*, an insightful book on prayer. But his old routines slowly began to change as his health deteriorated. He found less ability for other activities, so he spent a lot of time with friends or rereading his favorite books and authors: the *Odyssey* and the *Iliad*, Plato, Wordsworth, Herbert, Jane Austen, Dickens, Trollope, Sir Walter Scott. As long as possible, he continued to meet with the remaining Inklings at The Eagle and Child, sharing laughs, memories, and arguing over literature and theology.

He died on November 22, 1963, the same day John F. Kennedy was assassinated and famous British author Aldous Huxley died. Warren describes the final hours:

> *Friday, 22 November 1963, began much as other days: there was breakfast, then letters and the crossword puzzle. After lunch he fell asleep in his chair: I suggested that he would be more comfortable in bed, and he went there. At four I took his tea and found him drowsy but comfortable. Our few words then were the last: at five-thirty I heard a crash and ran in, to find him lying unconscious at the foot of his bed. He ceased to breathe some three or four minutes later.*[89]

The shock occasioned by Kennedy's assassination overshadowed the death of this humble English professor, but his lasting legacy is arguably far greater. His funeral was attended by only a few close friends and was missed by Warren, who was too devastated by loss to attend the ceremony. He stayed in bed all day, shaken by grief. A phrase from Shakespeare was inscribed on Jack's tombstone: "Men must endure their going hence." But Lewis did more than endure it. His life was lived in preparation for eternity and in a desire to fulfill the longings that had been with him since he was a child. Richard Ladborough, who saw Lewis just a week before his death, knew that the time was short.

> *"I somehow felt it was the last time we should meet, and when he escorted me, with his usual courtesy, to the door, I think he felt so too. Never was a man better prepared."*[90]

The legacy Lewis left behind is a rich one indeed—a long list of books, which not only show evidence of a firm commitment to orthodoxy, but also a scintillating wit, a logical mind and an ever-fresh imagination. He was a man surrendered to God, in love with life, and ready to share all that he could with others. Here was a fine example of the Christian life in action.

# C. S. Lewis:
## His Thought

# THE LONGING

*"You would not have called to me*
*unless I had been calling to you,"*
*said the Lion.*[91]

*L*ewis wrote often of an experience we have all had from time to time: the feeling that this life is somehow haunted by realities beyond it. It comes unbidden, often when we least expect it. It is a feeling of intense longing for something which lies beyond our grasp. Many call it nostalgia, or refer to it as romanticism or mysticism. Sometimes it comes as a feeling of ecstatic wonder. At other times, it is a melancholy to which we can ascribe no definite cause. Though it tends to produce such heightened emotional responses, it also produces a feeling of alienation and isolation, because what we long for is ultimately beyond us. Even as we experience this feeling, we know that it is transitory and will soon pass.

By his own admission, Lewis was a congenital romantic. Even before he was six years old, the sight of the Castlereagh Hills from his nursery window would cause a beautiful aching, an inconsolable longing to arise within his heart.

"They were not very far off but they were, to children, quite unobtainable. They taught me longing…"[92] These same feelings were activated by the memory, while standing one morning in the garden, of a toy garden Warren had given him in the nursery several years before. It also rose unbidden in the reading of a Beatrix Potter story and later in the reading of Longfellow's translation of an Icelandic epic. Great art, powerful literature, or the beauties of nature—any of these could be the trigger for Lewis' feelings of longing. Analyzing these experiences, Lewis found that their common quality was "an unsatisfied desire which is itself more desirable than any other satisfaction."[93]

But what was it that he was longing for? He had a powerful clue, while still an atheist, when he happened upon George MacDonald's book, *Phantastes*. In Lewis' mind, this book made the first connection between his feeling of longing and the Christian religion. Though he was not converted at the time, the book had the effect, as he put it, of baptizing his imagination.[94] It awakened for Lewis the sense of the numinous, of a reality that lay beyond the material realm we can experience with our senses.

The existence of this longing is evidence that there is more to life than we can see, touch, feel, smell or taste. There is no experience in this life that completely fulfills the desire it awakens within us. All we get are hints and guesses. Sometimes we feel like we are closing in on it; perhaps in a breathtaking vista of nature which seems to draw us in, or the silent peacefulness that comes over us when we stare up into the jeweled night sky. Could such dreams of glory as we dream be just a chance outcome of the evolutionary process? Or could it be that such experiences draw us to look beyond them? As Lewis queried, "Do fish complain of the sea for being wet? Or if they did, would that fact itself not strongly suggest that they had not always been, or would not always be, purely aquatic creatures? If you are really a product of a materialistic universe, how is it that you don't feel at home there?"[95] Or, he suggests in *Mere Christianity*, "If I find in myself a desire which no experience in this world can satisfy, the most probable explanation is that I was made for another world."[96]

This argument for the reality of heaven is one of Lewis' most potent arguments for the validity of the Christian view of life, though it is not an argument to be carried on in our brain, but one that touches the heart. It appeals to an instinctual or intuitional realization that lies within each of us. "Aha!" we say as we listen to Lewis' logic, "I know exactly what he means. I have felt it too." The service that Lewis provides is to unfold to us what it means. The heart is our homing pigeon flying through the darkness of the night toward our true home in God. As Augustine wrote: "Our hearts are restless until they rest in Thee."

Inherent within the longing is the reality that someday we shall have that which we have longed for. "There have been times when I think we do not desire heaven," Lewis wrote, "but more often I find myself wondering whether, in our heart of hearts, we have ever desired anything else…All your life an unattainable ecstasy has hovered just beyond the grasp of your consciousness. The day is coming when you will wake to find, beyond all hope, that you have attained it, or else, that it was within your reach and you have lost it forever."[97]

Ultimately, this longing promises a coming fulfillment almost too great to be imagined.

*If we take the imagery of Scripture seriously, if we believe that God will one day give us the Morning Star and cause us to put on the splendour of the sun, then we may surmise that both the ancient myths and the modern poetry, so false as history, may be very near the truth as prophecy. At present we are on the outside of the world, the wrong side of the door. We discern the freshness and purity of morning, but they do not make us fresh and pure. We cannot mingle with the splendours we see. But all the leaves of the New Testament are rustling with the rumor that it will not always be so. Someday, God willing, we shall get in. When human souls have become as perfect in voluntary obedience as the inanimate creation is in its lifeless obedience, then they will put on its glory, or rather that greater glory of which nature is only the first sketch.*[98]

# THE REALITY OF GOD

*There comes a moment when the children who have been playing burglars hush suddenly: was that a real footstep in the hall? There comes a moment when people who have been dabbling in religion ('Man's search for God'!) suddenly draw back. Suppose we really found Him? We never meant to come to that! Worse still, supposing He had found us?*[99]

Throughout history men and women have filled pages or filled the air with words about God. But for all the discussion, all the theorizing and theologizing, and all the poetic sentiment, most in our culture still do not know the reality of God. Lewis knew that although people might know *about* God, they must come to *know* God, to encounter Him as a person.

One of Lewis' clear teachings is that God is a Person. When you encounter God you are not "faced with an argument which demands your assent, but with a Person who demands your confidence."[100] Lewis points out that this is why so many are prone to dismiss the picture of God in the Old Testament, of Yahweh thundering away in judgment, being jealous of the other gods His people went after, and speaking with Moses on the mountain. Such a God is simply too concrete for our human tastes. We are more comfortable with the abstract.

People want an impersonal God, one who is non-threatening, who asks nothing of them and makes no claim upon their lives, thoughts or affections. Best of all is to conceive of God as some sort of "life force," a power source which we can tap—and therefore turn off and on like a faucet. But this simply will not do. God is utterly concrete. He is not an idea, a concept, a philosophy or a symbol. He is real. As Lewis put it, He is a fact. "God is basic Fact or Actuality, the source of all other facthood."[101]

This God has not left us without an awareness of His reality. Lewis points out four fundamental ways that God has revealed Himself to mankind. First, is the conscience which He built into our very nature. Second, He has, from the beginning, sent "good dreams"—those hope-filled stories in the pagan religions, about a god who dies and comes back to life. Third, He has revealed Himself in the life of the nation of Israel and through the Incarnation of God in Christ. Fourth, this revelation has been recorded in the Scriptures for our enlightenment.

While some might say that this is all a matter of unverifiable history and does not relate to us today, Lewis contends that we are not left to depend on the past alone. God is real in the present and we are without excuse. He has not left us to search blindly in the dark in an attempt to find Him. To the open heart, He is everywhere accessible.

*To some, God is discoverable everywhere; to others, nowhere. Those who do not find Him on*

> *earth are unlikely to find Him in space…But*
> *send a saint up in a spacecraft and he'll find*
> *God in space as he found God on the earth.*
> *Much depends upon the seeing eye.*[102]

It is true that God's presence is all around us, but the pantheist, who believes that everything around us **is** God, has grasped a truth and distorted it. God is not everything that surrounds us, but He can be seen in everything around us. We should never confuse the Creator with His creation, yet His reality is mirrored in creation to anyone who is open to the truth. In *Letters to Malcolm*, Lewis writes, "We may ignore, but we can nowhere evade, the presence of God. The world is crowded with Him. He walks everywhere incognito."[103]

The primary message of God's revelation of Himself is that He loves us. In *The Four Loves*, we see that God did not create us because He needed us, but out of the abundance of His desire to love. He is "Love Himself, the inventor of all loves."[104] His love is part of His nature, of the outflow of His goodness. "God loves us; not because we are lovable but because He is love, not because he needs to receive but because He delights to give."[105] But our confidence in God's love should never allow us to take Him lightly. It is at our own peril that we treat with casualness or indifference the weightiest of eternal matters.

> *God is the only comfort, He is also the supreme*
> *terror: the thing we most need and the thing we*
> *most want to hide from. He is our only possible*
> *ally, and we have made ourselves His enemies.*
> *Some people talk as if meeting the gaze of*
> *absolute goodness would be fun. They need to*
> *think again. They are still only playing with*
> *religion.*[106]

Most of us want the comfort of a God of grace and mercy without taking into account His holiness. We want a God who exists for our benefit, and whose highest goal is our happiness and security.

> *We want, in fact, not so much a Father in Heaven as a grandfather in heaven—a senile benevolence who, as they say, "liked to see young people enjoying themselves" and whose plan for the universe was simply that it might be said at the end of each day, "a good time was had by all."* [107]

This is one of the great accomplishments of Lewis' writing: to hold together these two aspects of God's character: His merciful love and His majestic holiness. In God's great love for us He wants to make us more lovable, but His holiness is such that He will not rest until our characters are perfected. He is willing to sacrifice all our present comforts to make us into new creations. His love "is not wearied by our sins, or our indifference; and therefore, it is quite relentless in its determination that we shall be cured of those sins, at whatever cost to us, at whatever cost to Him." [108]

"He is all a burning joy and a strength," says one of the characters in Perelandra. [109] Throughout his writing, both fiction and non-fiction, Lewis provides us memorable pictures of God and of the paradoxes of His character: majestic vulnerability and holy gaiety. Fictional creations like Aslan, the Emperor-over-the-sea, Maledil, and the Landlord remind us of how complex the truth about God is, and also how simple. As Colin Duriez writes so memorably:

> *We often make a basic mistake when trying to imagine God as unchangeable, invisible, infinite*

*and eternal. We are prone to miss his over-
whelming life, energy, joy and concreteness, to
fall into the folly of conceiving him as less definite than ourselves.*[110]

# WHO IS JESUS CHRIST?

*"Yes," said Queen Lucy. "In our world too, a Stable once had something inside it that was bigger than our whole world."*[111]

C. S. Lewis' faith was based on the surprising reality of the incarnation: that God Himself took on human form and came to live among us, ultimately dying for our sins. As a student of the great mythologies of the world, Lewis was familiar with the theme of a dying god who is raised to life again. What drew him to Christianity was his growing conviction that in the life, death, and resurrection of Jesus, this myth had become fact, that the dream of the pagan religions had actually happened when God took on human flesh and then died for our atonement. The incarnation was not just a beautiful thought, but an historical reality.

Under the pressure of a growing secular worldview, many theologians in Lewis' day, had given up on the orthodox interpretation of the nature of Jesus. They saw Him as a great teacher and a wise man, but certainly not as God in the flesh. Lewis believed, however, that this was the key doctrine of the

Christian faith. "The central miracle asserted by Christians," he wrote, "is the Incarnation." It is "the Grand Miracle."[112] And the purpose of this Grand Miracle is to do for us what we could never do for ourselves:

> *But supposing God became a man—suppose our human nature which can suffer and die was amalgamated with God's nature in one person—then that person could help us. He could surrender His will, and suffer and die, because He was God….But we cannot share God's dying unless God dies; and He cannot die except by being a man. That is the sense in which He pays our debt, and suffers for us what He Himself need not suffer at all.*[113]

Those who are not comfortable with the idea that God has become incarnate in the person of Jesus Christ will often try to dodge the ultimate question of His nature by concentrating on His giftedness as a teacher. Some are willing to conceive of Him as a great religious genius, applauding His high ethical demands upon humanity, and cheering His concern for justice and righteousness. And certainly, Jesus was one of the greatest ethicists and moral philosophers who ever lived. But if this is all we understand of Jesus, we have failed to truly understand Him.

To put Jesus on the same level with Mohammed, Confucius, or Buddha is not one of the options left open to us. By the claims He made, He significantly parted company with those whom we would consider great moral teachers. He claimed to be something more than that. He claimed to be God in the flesh. If He is not who He said He was, then He was either an evil liar or a crazy person.

> *I am trying here to prevent anyone from saying*
> *the really foolish thing that people often say*
> *about Him: "I'm ready to accept Jesus as a great*
> *moral teacher, but I don't accept His claim to*
> *be God." This is the one thing we must not say.*
> *A man who was merely a man and said the*
> *sort of things Jesus said would not be a great*
> *moral teacher. He would be a lunatic—on a*
> *level with the man who says he is a poached*
> *egg—or else he would be the Devil of Hell. You*
> *can shut Him up for a fool, you can spit at*
> *Him and kill Him as a demon; or you can fall*
> *at His feet and call Him Lord and God. But let*
> *us not come with any patronising nonsense*
> *about His being a great teacher. He has not left*
> *that open to us. He did not intend to.*[114]

Our options are exhausted: is He a liar, a lunatic, or is He the Lord?

Throughout his recorded words, Jesus does not point people to His teachings or philosophy. He points them to Himself as Savior. "Come unto Me," he says. His emphasis is not so much on believing in the ideas He espoused, as on trusting in Him. Our posture toward Christ is not merely an intellectual assent, but a surrender to His will. He not only wants to rescue us from sin, but to remake us into the people that He wants us to be. "In Christ," Lewis writes, "a new kind of man appeared: and the new kind of life which began in Him is to be put into us."[115]

One of the most powerful portraits ever drawn of Jesus, appears in *The Chronicles of Narnia*. In these mythical tales, Aslan is a great lion who gives his life to right the wrong that has intruded into his world. Aslan is the answer to the question of what Christ might be like if He entered a world like Narnia to redeem it from evil. Many have found themselves strangely drawn to Lewis' Christ-like lion.

But Aslan is not a tame lion. It involves risk on the part of the children to even approach him. Like Christ, he cannot be bargained with. They must trust and surrender.

> *"Are you not thirsty?" said the Lion.*
>
> *"I'm dying of thirst," said Jill.*
>
> *"Then drink," said the Lion.*
>
> *"May I—could I—would you mind going away while I do?" said Jill.*
>
> *The Lion answered this only by a look and a very low growl. And as Jill gazed at its motionless bulk, she realized that she might as well have asked the whole mountain to move aside for her convenience.*
>
> *The delicious rippling noise of the stream was driving her nearly frantic.*
>
> *"Will you promise not to—do anything to me, if I do come?" said Jill.*
>
> *"I make no promise," said the Lion.*
>
> *Jill was so thirsty now that, without noticing it, she had come a step nearer.*
>
> *"Do you eat girls?" she said.*
>
> *"I have swallowed up girls and boys, women and men, kings and emperors, cities and realms," said the Lion. It didn't say this as if it were boasting, not as if it were sorry, nor as if it were angry. It just said it.*
>
> *"I daren't come and drink," said Jill.*
>
> *"Then you will die of thirst," said the Lion.*
>
> *"Oh dear!" said Jill, coming another step nearer.*

*"I suppose I must go and look for another
stream then."*
*"There is no other stream," said the Lion.*[116]

Perhaps Lewis best summarizes his views on Jesus Christ
in his response to the important question, "What are we to
make of Christ?"

> *There is no question of what we can make of
> Him, it is entirely a question of what He
> intends to make of us. You must accept or
> reject the story.*[117]

This Christ, who accomplished so much for mankind, was
the center of both Lewis' life and writings.

# FAITH AND THE INTELLECT

*When you are arguing against Him you are arguing against the very power that makes you able to argue at all.*[118]

"Everyone has warned me," Lewis writes at the beginning of a discussion of the meaning and significance of the doctrine of the Trinity, "not to tell you what I am going to tell you…They all say 'the ordinary reader does not want Theology; give him plain practical religion.' I have rejected their advice. I do not think the ordinary reader is such a fool. Theology means 'the science of God,' and I think any man who wants to think about God at all would like to have the clearest and most accurate ideas about Him which are available."[119]

One of the truisms of the modern era is that "religion is a matter of the heart." Lewis would reject this truism as simply not true. Although the heart is certainly involved in embracing and practicing our faith, it is the whole man that must come to God, and that includes the mind. Our faith in God should not be based only upon our experiences or desires, but upon a firmly held intellectual conviction that we have found the truth.

Likewise, the unbeliever cannot simply dismiss Christianity out of hand as foolishness that appeals only to the ignorant. As Lewis points out, the evidence cannot be so weak as to warrant the view that believers are indifferent to evidence. We know from the history of thought that this is not true. Many of the most powerful minds of the past in both the arts and the sciences were committed believers. "We may suppose them to have been mistaken, but we must suppose the error was at least plausible."[120]

For Lewis, becoming a Christian was the result of a long and careful intellectual journey. As a young man, he was quick to embrace any argument that might throw doubt upon the veracity of the Christian message, but as he matured he found himself faced with increasing evidence that the seemingly unlikely gospel message was, in fact, the truth. He was not predisposed to Christianity, nor did he have a religious temperament. "I'm not the religious type," he would insist, but he was led to the Christian faith because it most fully answered to the facts. In *Surprised by Joy*, he is adamant about the reluctance surrounding his conversion; he didn't believe because he wanted it to be true, but was compelled to believe because all the evidence pointed in that direction.

Because he came to faith by this path, Lewis does not employ sentimental salesmanship or emotional appeals in his writings. He does not use tricks to move us, but wishes to convince us of the truth. "I am not asking anyone to accept Christianity if his best reasoning is against it," he wrote.[121] And once we have come to believe, we are not asked to jettison the thinking process.

> *The American in the old story defined Faith as*
> *"the power of believing what we know to be*

> *untrue." Now I define Faith as the power of con-*
> *tinuing to believe what we once honestly*
> *thought to be true until cogent reasons for hon-*
> *estly changing our minds are brought before*
> *us.*[122]

Because of his conviction that our intellect is an important element in our faith, Lewis tried throughout his writings
to provide reasonable answers to the questions and struggles
many people face in becoming or remaining Christians. He
gave a high place to reason and its importance in human life,
because all knowledge, he argued, depends on the validity of
being able to reason our way to the truth.

Because so many fail to see that the Christian faith is a
logical and intellectually compelling belief system, believers
must not neglect to emphasize that whatever else you value
about Christianity—its inspiring message, its comforting
promises, its social usefulness, its moral strength—you must
always communicate that it is the Truth.

> *One of the great difficulties is to keep before the*
> *audience's mind the question of Truth. They*
> *always think you are recommending*
> *Christianity not because it is true but because*
> *it is good. And in the discussion they will at*
> *every moment try to escape from the issue*
> *"True—or False" into stuff about a good soci-*
> *ety, or morals, or the incomes of Bishops, or the*
> *Spanish Inquisition, or France, or Poland—or*
> *anything whatever. You have to keep forcing*
> *them back, and back again, to the real*
> *point…One must keep on pointing out that*
> *Christianity is a statement which, if false, is of*

> *no importance, and if true, of infinite impor-*
> *tance. The one thing it cannot be is moderately*
> *important.*[123]

And so, throughout his books, Lewis argues vigorously for the fact that Christianity gives the best and most logical explanation for human life as we know and experience it. Along the way, he never becomes dogmatic, but keeps a good sense of humor and does not set himself up as an infallible expert. He never tries to dazzle his readers with academic jargon or asks them to blindly accept his authority. Instead, he asks his readers to think along with him, taking them step by step through his arguments, anticipating their objections, and concentrating on "mere Christianity" rather than any particular denominational brand name.

Lewis challenges us to think for ourselves and not to leave the practice of theology to the experts. Understanding the doctrines of our faith is important because they provide us with a map for thinking and keep us from being limited by our own spiritual experiences or from wandering off into a private esoteric religion that we have invented for ourselves. Theology is simply thinking rightly about God, fulfilling the Biblical mandate to "love God with all our mind." If we can do this we can show others what is at stake in the important message that the Christian has to share with the world. We can be fearless in proclaiming that Christianity is not a collection of nice ideas, but is the truth.

> *Here is a door, behind which, according to*
> *some people, the secret of the universe is wait-*
> *ing for you. Either that's true, or it isn't. And if*
> *it isn't, then what the door really conceals is*
> *simply the greatest fraud, the most colossal*

"sell" on record. Isn't it obviously the job of every man (that is a man and not a rabbit) to try to find out which, and then to devote his full energies either to serving this tremendous secret or to exposing and destroying this gigantic humbug?[124]

# PAIN

*"God whispers to us in our pleasures, speaks in our conscience, but shouts in our pains: it is His megaphone to rouse a deaf world."*[125]

*A*ll arguments in justification of suffering provoke bitter resentment against the author. You would like to know how I behave when I am experiencing pain, not writing books about it."[126] These words are from one of the first books Lewis wrote after his conversion, *The Problem of Pain*, an honest and forthright discussion of pain and the role it plays in our lives. Of course it is always dangerous to write about pain; many in fact, find it presumptuous.

But when he spoke of pain and its place in our lives, Lewis was writing of experiences with which he was well familiar. He had known pain throughout his life, both physical and emotional. Not only the usual succession of colds and flu, aches and pains, toothaches, and weariness of the body, but also the loss of his mother while still a young child, suffering life-threatening wounds in the First World War, the loss of a beloved wife, and the slow decay of his body in old age.

He claimed no special courage when it came to dealing with pain ("If I knew any way of escape I would crawl through sewers to find it."[127]), but he did believe that our pains could be redemptive and bring growth and maturity to our lives.

As a young atheist, Lewis felt that the existence of pain was one of the strongest arguments **against** the existence of a loving God. If God was both all-powerful and good, why did He not eliminate pain from the universe? Later reflection on this question helped Lewis to see that pain is an integral part of a universe which reflects human free will. Could God both protect a person from pain and at the same time allow him free will? It seems not. Most of our pain is at least partially the result of our own foolish choices. Other kinds of pain are more mysterious, but seem to fit somehow into God's plan.

Suffering for its own sake is never good and we should try to do all we can to alleviate it in the lives of others. But pain is important because it wakens us from the illusion that all is well in the universe. It reminds us that we are a fallen race living in a fallen world and that we need help from outside ourselves to heal the effects of our fallenness. This is why Lewis called pain a megaphone to rouse a deaf world.

Lewis believed that we can, in a very real sense, participate in the sufferings of Christ by embracing our pains and difficulties for His sake. As he wrote to an American lady:

> *We are told that even those tribulations which fall on us by necessity, if embraced for Christ's sake, become as meritorious as voluntary sufferings and every missed meal can be converted into a fast if taken in the right way.*[128]

Sometimes, he says, we cannot be trusted with lives of pleasure and security. For when we possess these, we so quickly forget the giver of all good things, and trust in the gifts instead. "How few of us He dare send happiness because He knows we will forget Him if He gives any sort of nice things for the moment."[129]

We are mistaken, writes Lewis, if we consider this world as some sort of grand hotel where our purpose is to find unending pleasure. We should never think that pain is unusual or extraordinary. Instead, we should see this world as a training ground for eternity. "If you think of this world as a place intended simply for our happiness, you find it quite intolerable: think of it as a place of training and correction and it's not so bad."[130] Sometimes we don't realize how good we have it.

We are like the cat who sees the trip to the veterinarian as a terrifying and cruel event, when it may be just what it needs to save its life. God uses the difficult and trying things in our lives to build our character. As Paul writes in the eighth chapter of Romans, "All things work together for the good for those who are in Christ Jesus." This is our great hope: that God has a vision for the kind of person He wants us to be and will use any means necessary to make that vision a reality, even at the the cost of our discomfort.

One of the strengths of Lewis' character is his honesty, and this is especially obvious in his mature writing. If some readers of his early book, *The Problem of Pain* might accuse him of being a little too self-assured and having all the answers, a look at his later book, *A Grief Observed*, shows his brutal honesty about the hurts and doubts which troubled him after the loss of his wife. In fact, the discomfort of publishing such an honest journal of his struggles and questionings was what caused him to release the book under the pseudonym N. W. Clerk. Ironically, many people sent copies of the book to Lewis, thinking it would be of help to him in his time of loneliness and bereavement!

Lewis believed that we could be a real help to others in their time of pain and that our help could go beyond our sympathetic feelings. We could, he believed, actually take upon ourselves some of the sufferings of others. At first, this was simply an idea he had taken from his friend Charles Williams, who called it "coinherence." But an event in his life confirmed for him that it was not just an idea, but a reality. When Joy was recovering from her initial bout with cancer, her bones were brittle, riddled with cancer, and in need of calcium. During her recovery, Lewis began to experience great pain in his own bones. When the doctor checked him, it was found that he was losing calcium from his bones at the same time as it was being replenished in Joy's. He was convinced that he had been allowed to take her pain into his own legs and carry some of the weight of her illness.

Lewis could no more solve the "problem of pain" than any human being could. Pain will always remain one of the mysterious elements of our human existence. What Lewis did, however, was to point us to God's redemptive purposes at work in our sufferings, as well as the promise of His presence in our time of need.

# Miracles

*The miracles in fact are a retelling in small letters of the very same story which is written across the whole world in letters too large for some of us to see.*[131]

*M*any theologians in Lewis' time were committed to the ethical system which Jesus taught and the example of His life, but drew the line at the belief that there was a realm beyond what could be experienced with the senses. They rejected the idea of a supernatural reality that could impinge upon or affect our world. For these thinkers, Jesus was a good teacher, but He could not have been born of a virgin or resurrected from the dead. But Lewis saw clearly that to remove such elements from the Christian faith was to strip it of its distinctive message and leave it as a toothless moralism.

The reason that some accept the supernatural while others reject it, is that people differ in their fundamental ideas about the universe. Lewis pointed to two basic views of reality. The first is that of Materialism, the belief that nature is all that there is, that it is the "whole show." There is nothing beyond what can be perceived by the five senses. If we cannot touch, taste, feel, smell or hear it, it cannot be a reality and only exists in our heads. Thus, God, angels, the soul and heaven are merely psychological wishes, not concrete realities. If this is true, to seek evidence for miracles is as silly as looking for Santa Claus. The other major view of reality is that of Supernaturalism, the belief that the universe is a dependent creation of an almighty God, who made it out of nothing and can invade the material realm, which He stands above, at will.

Some might object to the supernatural view by pointing to the fact that we can explain away everything that falls into the category of a miracle. There are, they would say, logical explanations that make supernatural ones unnecessary. However, as Lewis points out, hypothetical answers and possible explanations do not necessarily constitute the truth, they merely reflect our presuppositions about the universe.

> *Every event which might claim to be a miracle is, in the last resort, something presented to our senses, something seen, heard, touched, smelled, or tasted. And our senses are not infallible. If anything extraordinary seems to have happened, we can always say that we have been the victims of an illusion. If we hold a philosophy which excludes the supernatural, this is what we always shall say. What we learn from experience depends on the kind of philosophy we bring to experience.*[132]

If naturalism is true, then miracles are impossible. And many hold to this belief on the basis that it is the modern scientific way to think. Lewis struggled against the views of those who felt that belief in miracles was somehow old-fashioned and who rejected them asserting that modern men had outgrown such ideas. If we have rejected the supernatural on the basis of evidence, what is that evidence? Lewis helps us to see that the rejection of the miraculous is a matter of choice rather than of evidence.

Part of the problem is that we see miracles as breaking the laws of nature. But miracles do not break any natural laws, for God, who is the originator of the miracle, is the author of the laws. "If God creates a miraculous spermatozoon in the body of a virgin, it does not proceed to break any laws. The laws take over at once. Nature is ready. Pregnancy follows, according to all the normal laws, and nine months later a child is born."[133] The miraculous always accommodates the laws of nature.

> *Miraculous wine will intoxicate, miraculous conception will lead to pregnancy, inspired books will suffer all the ordinary processes of textual corruption, miraculous bread will be digested. The divine art of miracle is not an art of suspending the pattern to which events conform but of feeding new events into that pattern.*[134]

So then, we cannot reject miracles simply because we seldom experience them or because they are unpopular to the modern mind. The only basis we have for rejecting miracles is if we believe in the materialistic worldview of naturalism.

Lewis suggests that we can reject naturalism for two reasons. First, because it undermines the validity of thought itself, and second, because it provides no basis for the moral sentiments that we universally hold.

Naturalism undermines the validity of thought itself because, if naturalism is true, then all thinking is just the result of chemical reactions occurring in the brain. If thinking is not a participation in the reason of God, it has no objective basis on which to test its truthfulness. How do we know that those chemical reactions are producing anything more than illusions? Is it valid to use our thought processes to reject any real objective basis for thinking? As Lewis wrote, "When you are arguing against Him you are arguing against the very power that makes you able to argue at all: it is like cutting off the branch you are sitting on."[135]

Naturalism provides no basis for moral sentiments, because, once again, if there is no basis outside of this world from which to judge moral questions, then morality is simply a matter of subjective choice. Writing at a time when the Nazis were bringing terror to all of Europe, Lewis pointed to the fact that without a real Moral Law that exists outside our material world, we have no basis for saying that they are wrong in their actions and we are morally right. Morality is reduced to a matter of preference. "It seems, then, we are forced to believe in a real Right and Wrong. People may sometimes be mistaken about them, just as people sometimes get their sums wrong; but they are not a matter of mere taste and opinion any more than the multiplication table."[136]

Believing in the supernatural and in the possibility of miracles, helps us to make sense out of our otherwise inexplicable human experience. God does not invade nature willy-nilly and thus we do not see miracles happen every day. For God respects and works within the natural order He created. But it is a glorious truth to know that He does, on occasion, invade our reality in order to bring benefit and help to His people.

# Mythology and the Gospel

*God sent the human race what I call good dreams: I*
*mean those queer stories scattered all through the*
*heathen religions about a god who dies and comes*
*to life again, and by his death has somehow given*
*new life to men.*[137]

In recent years, the study of mythology, driven by the work of Joseph Campbell and Mircea Eliade, has become the focus of great popular curiosity. But long before this renaissance of interest, Lewis found, in the study of mythology, a fascinating window into understanding the spiritual longings of humanity. Unlike Joseph Campbell, whose conception of myth led him to believe in a radical form of religious pluralism wherein all religions are the same, Lewis connected his study of myth to his Christian commitment.

For many modern people, the word "myth" means something that is untrue or false. But Lewis placed great value on myths, and the making of mythical stories, as one of humanity's primary forms of communicating truth and apprehending reality.

Myth is important to humans because it is a way of expressing the inexpressible. In using myth, Lewis says, "we come nearest to experiencing as a concrete what can otherwise be understood only as an abstraction."[138] Myth is an archetypal tale which reflects and signifies eternal realities. It is a "real though unfocused gleam of divine truth falling on human imagination" which allows the mysterious to be articulated.[139] Like the allegory, its near cousin in literary form, it reaches after "some transcendental reality which the forms of discursive thought cannot contain."[140]

Myth goes beyond allegory in that it cannot be reduced to simple one-for-one relationships between the symbol and what it stands for. Myth symbolizes something that cannot be reduced to a concept. In the framing of the story, myth takes on truths which might seem dogmatic and abstract in simple discursive explanation, and makes them into functioning realities.

Because it has the power to personalize the message, myths break through our limitations and intellectual objections. Before God's revelation of Himself in Christ, the myths of ancient peoples served as pointers to the truth. They revealed inklings of God's character and existence. Some have pointed to common themes in the world's mythologies and used this as evidence against the uniqueness of Christianity, but Lewis saw these themes in a much different way. These pagan myths Lewis calls "good dreams," for they provide imperfect guesses and hints of what God's relationship is to humanity. It was this dawning understanding of the relationship of the ancient myths to Christianity that overcame many of Lewis' initial objections to faith. As he wrote to Arthur Greeves, "the story of Christ is simply a true myth: a myth working on us in the same way as the others, but with this tremendous difference: *that it really happened.*"[141] However, God did not leave humanity with this imperfect understanding.

The incarnation of God in Christ became the culmination of man's mythic desires.

> *Now as myth transcends thought, Incarnation transcends myth. The heart of Christianity is a myth which is also a fact. The old myth of the Dying God, without ceasing to be a myth comes down from the heaven of legend and imagination to the earth of history. It happens—at a particular time, at a particular place, followed by definable historical consequences. We pass from a Balder or an Orisis, dying nobody knows when or where, to a historical person crucified (it is all in order) under Pontius Pilate. By becoming fact it does not cease to be a myth: that is the miracle.*[142]

As the title of this essay from *God in the Dock* suggests, "Myth Became Fact." But, becoming historical does not reduce the imaginative impact of the incarnation. It still beckons to our imagination, our emotions and our hearts.

This being the case, myth addresses contemporary society in a way that logical argumentation cannot. It has a way of breaking past our barriers of unbelief and affecting us very deeply. As Lewis wrote, it can arouse in us sensations we have never had before, never anticipated having, as though we had broken out of our normal mode of consciousness and "possessed joys not promised to our birth." It gets under our skin, hits us at a level deeper than our thoughts or even our passions, troubles oldest certainties till all questions are re-opened, and in general shocks us more fully awake than we are for most of our lives.[143]

Sensing this power for communication, Lewis made extensive use of myth in his books. He remythologized, creating new myths or dressing old ones in new forms. This was the manner in which Lewis was able to draw reason and imagination together as a functioning unit. This indeed seems to be the way that God speaks to humanity, so why should it not be a sensible form of human communication? The manner in which Lewis ended his essay on "Myth Become Fact" suggests a way for the creative artist to communicate eternal realities and preserve eternal traditions.

> *If God chooses to be mythopoeic...shall we refuse to be mythopathic? For this is the marriage of heaven and earth: Perfect Myth and Perfect Fact [the Incarnation]: claiming not only our love and our obedience, but also our wonder and delight, addressed to the savage, the child, and the poet in each one of us no less than to the moralist, the scholar, and the philosopher.*[144]

Lewis himself was one of the finest mythopoeic writers of the twentieth century. In his science fiction trilogy, in his children's series *The Chronicles of Narnia*, in *The Great Divorce*, and especially in *Till We Have Faces*, Lewis crafted tales that reach beyond mere storytelling and reveal to us deep truths about the world God has made. He did this by reflecting this world in the fictional ones he created. Lewis was a master at remythologizing the gospel story. By presenting Christian truths in new and unfamiliar settings, he gave a freshness and urgency to the gospel message. In so doing, he challenges us to find new ways to express the eternal and timeless truth.

# The Heart of a Child

*People [have] no particular ages in Aslan's country–
Even in this world, of course, it is the stupidest
children who are the most childish and the stupidest
grown-ups who are most grown-up.*[145]

In many ways it would be hard to imagine a more unlikely candidate for being a classic children's writer than C. S. Lewis. He never married or had children of his own until very late in life, when he became a husband to Joy and step-father to her children. Previous to that, his experience with children was limited both by his lifestyle and his tastes. In 1935, he wrote to Arthur Greeves: "I theoretically hold that one ought to like children, but am shy with them in practice."[146] A few years later, in the first chapter of *The Abolition of Man* he wrote, "I myself do not enjoy the society of small children."[147]

This attitude of discomfort with youngsters changed as Lewis grew older. More and more, he came to discover and accept the heart of the child hidden within this brilliant Oxford thinker.

*When I was ten, I read fairy tales in secret and
would have been ashamed if I had been found
doing so. Now that I am fifty I read them
openly. When I became a man I put away
childish things, including the fear of childish-
ness and the desire to be very grown up.*[148]

Certainly one of the qualities in Lewis' writing that so
endears him to his readers is his almost childlike sense of
wonder and enthusiasm for life. Like a child, Lewis loved the
simple things of life: a refreshing splash in the water, the company of a beloved pet, a rousing walk in nature. He refused to
complicate his life with unnecessary gadgets and technolo-
gies, but rather found great joy in letting his imagination take
flight.

Lewis celebrates the child-like spirit in many of his
works, but he differentiates being *child-like* from being *childish.* To be child-like is to exercise a simple trust in God. To be
childish is to avoid the responsibilities of life and refuse maturity. God wants us to have "a child's heart, but a grown-up's
head. He wants us to be simple, single-minded, affectionate,
and teachable, as good children are; but He also wants every
bit of intelligence we have to be alert at its job, and in first
class fighting trim."[149] Lewis quotes approvingly the apostle
Paul's admonition to be "harmless as doves, wise as serpents."
We earn no points with God for choosing to be ignorant.

Instead, to be child-like is to have a heart of openness and
trust toward our heavenly Father. In calling us to child-
likeness, Christ did not mean that the "processes of thought by which
people become Christians must be childish processes." Rather,
the spirit of a man must "become humble and trustful like a
child and, like a child, simple in motive."[150] As adults we
struggle so vigorously with false motives and corrupting attitudes in our lives. We must learn to put these aside to live in

honesty before God. We must learn to trust Him to meet our needs and to bring real meaning to our lives.

Lewis believed that the child could live on in the heart of the grown-up. Therefore, he appeals to the adult in children (he was always respectful to children and never spoke condescendingly to them) and to the children in adults. He tells a humorous anecdote which demonstrates the affinity between the child and the adult:

> *Once in a hotel dining-room I said, rather too loudly, 'I loathe prunes.' 'So do I,' came an unexpected six-year-old voice from another table. Sympathy was instantaneous. Neither of us thought it funny. We both knew that prunes are far too nasty to be funny. That is the proper meeting between man and child as independent personalities.*[151]

As we grow and mature, we sometimes become blinded to the important things of life, trapped into concern for the merely expedient. One of the glories of child-like simplicity is that it opens our eyes to see more clearly. In the second book of the *Chronicles of Narnia*, Lucy notes a difference in Aslan when she sees him again. "You're bigger," she exclaims. "Every year you grow, you will find me bigger," answers Aslan.[152] But to do so, she must keep her child-like trust.

Children use their imaginations in order to grow. In *Mere Christianity*, Lewis suggests how we might, as children, learn to "pretend" in order to mature, to act better than we know ourselves to be in the hope that we will become the kind of person for whom that right action would be natural.

> *Very often the only way to get a quality in reality is to start behaving as if you had it already.*

> *That is why children's games are so important.*
> *They are always pretending to be grown-ups—*
> *playing soldiers, playing shop. But all the time,*
> *they are hardening their muscles and sharpen-*
> *ing their wits, so that the pretense of being*
> *grown-ups helps them to grow up in earnest.*[153]

So it is that we must grow up with regard to responsibility, learning what is expected of us by God and endeavoring to become that kind of person. We must also exercise our intellects in obedience to Christ, not ignoring them but bringing them under His Lordship. But in our hearts we must never lose that simple trust and hope of the child within.

# A Life With Books

*You can't get a cup of tea large enough or a book long enough to suit me.*[154]

*B*ooks have played an important part in the lives of almost every great leader in history, and it is no surprise to find that they played such a significant role in the life of C. S. Lewis. Long before he made the study of literature his chosen profession, books had been a major part of his development. Even had he not become a university professor, it is clear that Lewis would have been a man who treasured reading. He read books of all kinds: fiction, poetry, theology, philosophy, history, and more. Colleagues remember him as a man who had read and digested just about everything. Lewis knew the value of books.

His love of books began early in life. He recalls, in his autobiography, his mother and father sitting in their comfortable chairs every evening engrossed in their latest book. He soon caught the passion. He describes how, as a child, he was surrounded by books:

*There were books in the study, books in the
drawing room, books in the cloakroom, books
(two deep) in the great bookcase on the landing, books in a bedroom, books piled as high as
my shoulder in the cistern attic, books of all
kinds reflecting every transient stage of my parents' interest, books readable and unreadable,
books suitable for a child and books most
emphatically not. Nothing was forbidden me. In
the seemingly endless rainy afternoons I took
volume after volume down from the shelves. I
had always the same certainty of finding a
book that was new to me as a man who walks
into a field has of finding a new blade of
grass.*[155]

As Lewis grew, his love of reading did not ebb. His early
correspondence with his friend, Arthur Greeves, is largely
taken up with the discussion of the books which each of them
were reading. It was only natural that several of the stages on
the way to his conversion were inaugurated by the reading of
a book that greatly affected him. As he later wrote, "a young
man who wishes to remain a sound atheist cannot be too
careful of his reading. There are traps everywhere. . ."[156]

Many of these traps lie in those old books which have so
profoundly affected our world. Lewis greatly valued the classics. He believed that it was the timeless books which are best
able to deal with the real issues of our own time. "The more
'up to date' the book is, the sooner it will be dated."[157] For that
reason, Lewis suggested spending the bulk of one's reading
time on those books that had established themselves as truly
worthy of attention. Instead of the latest additions to the bestseller lists, he recommended spending our reading time with

the time-honored greats. Many people steer clear of the classics for fear that they are irrelevant or too difficult. But the classics are neither. Granted, many of the classic books require a little more concentration than the latest fiction bestseller, but it is a concentration that will pay real dividends in terms of understanding. Not only do the great books help us to understand the past, they also awaken a deeper understanding of the present. That is why Lewis was adamant about people making the classics a part of their personal reading program. "It is a good rule, after reading a new book, never to allow yourself another new one till you have read an old one in between. If that is too much for you, you should at least read one old one for every three new ones."[158]

One of Lewis' passionate convictions about books was that the very best books need to be read and reread throughout one's life. It won't do to make your way through a book such as Dante's *Divine Comedy* and then check it off your list as an accomplishment on the way to being "well read." Lewis believed that we lose a great deal by only reading a book once. We must revisit the great books again and again throughout our lives, for they will always have something new to teach us. As he wrote, "The sure mark of an unliterary man is that he considers "I've read it already" to be a conclusive argument against reading a work…Those who read great works, on the other hand, will read the same work ten, twenty or thirty times during the course of their life."[159]

Lewis approached his reading as an adventure of discovery. He did not content himself with a cursory scanning of the pages, but instead carefully studied the books he read, marking significant passages and pausing to thoroughly understand their arguments. This was especially helpful with a more difficult book. In a letter to Arthur Greeves, Lewis describes how he made a book his own:

> *I begin by making a map on one of the end
> leafs: then I put in a genealogical tree or two.
> Then I put a running headline at the top of
> each page: finally I index at the end of all the
> passages I have for any reason underlined. I
> often wonder…why so few people make a
> hobby of their reading in this way. Many an
> otherwise dull book which I had to read have I
> enjoyed in this way, with a fine-nibbed pen in
> my hand: one is making something all the time
> and a book so read acquires the charm of a toy
> without losing that of a book.*[160]

Is it any wonder that a man who read so thoroughly was so brilliantly engaging and had such an astonishing grasp of so many issues?

One of the great pleasures of reading, as Lewis saw it, was to be able to discuss what he had read with others. As a young man he wrote to Arthur that "when one has read a book, I think there is nothing so nice as discussing it with someone else—even though it sometimes produces rather fierce arguments."[161] This was a conviction he held throughout his life. He reveled in the pleasure of intense discussion of a book with friends. To share a book in common was one of friendships greatest joys.

But there is another kind of "friendship" which we discover in good books—learning to see through the eyes of others. One of the great joys of reading is that we are ourselves expanded as we share in the insights of thoughtful people who have gone before us. As Lewis writes:

> *My own eyes are not enough for me; I will see
> through those of others…in reading great liter-
> ature I become a thousand men and yet remain*

> *myself. Like a night sky in the Greek poem, I see*
> *with a myriad eyes, but it is still I who see.*
> *Here, as in worship, in love, in moral action,*
> *and in knowing, I transcend myself; and am*
> *never more myself than when I do.*[162]

In his own life, Lewis demonstrated the powerful influence that books can have and his example remains a challenge for us today. The reading of good books will make us wiser, broaden our horizons, challenge our thinking, give flight to our imaginations, and provide hours of enjoyment. Where do we start? Perhaps we could do no better than repeat the advice Lewis gave to one of his students: "The great thing is to be always reading but not to get bored—treat it not like work, more as a vice! Your book bill ought to be your biggest extravagance."[163]

# FRIENDSHIP

*Friendship is unnecessary, like philosophy, like art, like the universe itself (for God did not need to create). It has no survival value; rather it is one of those things which give value to survival.*[164]

C. S. Lewis is almost alone among modern thinkers in the value he places on friendship. We talk so much about love and romantic attachments that often friendship is a quality of love which is little discussed. One of the distinctive characteristics in the life of Lewis was the number of close friendships he had and the great value that he placed on them. Perhaps he best summarized his opinions about friendship in a letter to one of his very closest friends: "Friendship is the greatest of worldly goods. Certainly to me it is the chief happiness of life. If I had to give a piece of advice to a young man about a place to live, I think I should say, 'sacrifice almost everything to live where you can be near your friends.' I know I am very fortunate in that respect."[165] He certainly was. Throughout his life, Lewis was surrounded by men and women with whom he could share his deepest feelings, argue his deepest prejudices, and share moments both quiet and riotous.

"Friendship," writes Lewis, "is born at the moment when one man says to another, 'What! You too? I thought that no one but myself. . .'"[166] He spoke from experience. One of his great life-long friendships, that with Arthur Greeves, was born on their discovering a common love for Norse mythology. This initial shared passion opened the door for them to share other enthusiasms and to learn new ones from each other. Lewis believed friendship was based on a commonality of interests, shared enjoyments, and meaningful conversation. While the primary concern of lovers is with each other and with their relationship, friends come together because of common values and interests. "We picture lovers face to face but friends side by side; their eyes look ahead."[167] To find those who share one's own joys is one of the greatest pleasures of life. "Friends are not primarily absorbed in each other. It is when we are doing things together that friendship springs up—painting, sailing ships, praying, philosophizing, fighting shoulder to shoulder."[168]

Lewis spent much time with his treasured friends. Several times a year he would organize walking tours of a few days duration where he and his companions could hike around the countryside, sharing laughs, stories, opinions and good fellowship. Often his brother, Warren, was a traveling companion. At other times it would be Owen Barfield, Arthur Greeves, J. R. R. Tolkien, or another of his friends.

Another source of wonderful revelry was the weekly meeting of the literary group who called themselves the Inklings. Sometimes meeting in Lewis' college rooms, other times at the local pub, they would read aloud the books and essays they were writing and give each other advice and criticism. Many of Lewis' most famous books were "premiered" at these informal gatherings, which included such friends as

Tolkien, Williams, Barfield, Coghill, Dyson, and Dr. Humphrey Havard. When you read the works of the various writers who numbered themselves among the Inklings, it is easy to see the influence they had upon each other.

Lewis not only had great friends, but was himself the most dependable of friends to others. As he became more famous later in life and began to reap the financial benefits of his notoriety, he gave large amounts of money away to needy friends and acquaintances. He was also always willing to lend a listening ear or commit himself to serious prayer for the needs which he could not meet himself.

Lewis believed that our modern world puts such emphasis on romantic love, that we denigrate the value of friendship. But if we fail to see the importance of friendship, we miss out on one of the greatest tools we have to help us, not only to enjoy our lives but also to grow in maturity and spiritual depth. Great friends help to broaden us and to challenge us to rise above our own limitations. "The next best thing to being wise oneself," wrote Lewis, "is to live in a circle of those who are."[169] And the very act of surrounding oneself with wise friends will expose us to the kind of encouragements and challenges that will help us become better people. Lewis learned the truth that is taught in Proverbs 27:9: "Oil and perfume make the heart glad, so a man's counsel is sweet to his friend." Good friends make good people better.

"Friendship exhibits a glorious 'nearness by resemblance' to Heaven itself"[170] because it is not affected by the jealousies that sometimes cloud romantic attachments. Friendship delights in the addition of the third or fourth party, who, if they too are friends, only heighten the enjoyment of an occasion. It is the unselfishness of friendship that is truly one of its glories.

But sometimes friendship will pass into the realm of romantic love. This is what happened to Lewis late in his life.

His relationship with Joy Davidman, at first a sharing of enthusiasms for literature and theology, eventually became a romantic love of extraordinary depth. Friendship is the best basis for a marriage. Infatuation with appearances, desire for the prestige that another can bring to us, the security of being wanted: all these things pass away in time. What remains is the ability to share warm moments of comradeship with a friend. What a glorious thing when a marriage can combine passion with depth of friendship.

We can learn much from Lewis about the necessity of developing true friendships. God has created us in such a way that we need each other and it is in the company of good friends that our character is perfected.

# HUMOR

*Laugh and fear not, creatures. Now that you are no
longer dumb and witless, you need not always be
grave. For jokes as well as justice come in with
speech.*[171]

Those who knew C. S. Lewis remember his vivid and
witty sense of humor as one of the great charms of his
personality. He was a man who cherished a good laugh and
was always ready with a quick comeback or a funny story.
Certainly one of the qualities that makes Lewis' books so
enjoyable is this fabulous sense of humor. "A little comic relief
in a discussion does no harm, however serious the topic may
be," he once wrote.[172] Lewis not only wrote these words, he
practiced them. All of his books, even works of serious literary criticism and theology are peppered with humor.

Lewis does not merely use humor to spice up his writing,
but allows humor to serve the purpose of illustrating a point
he is trying to make. In this classic example, Lewis uses his
wit to make a very serious point about the possibility of the
immortality of animals:

> *I have been warned not even to raise the question of animal immortality, lest I find myself 'in company with all the old maids.' I have no objection to the company. I do not think either virginity or old age contemptible…Nor am I greatly moved by jocular enquiries such as 'Where will you put all the mosquitoes?'—a question to be answered on its own level by pointing out that, if the worst came to the worst, a heaven for mosquitoes and a hell for men could be very conveniently be combined.*[173]

Like his father before him, Lewis loved to collect funny stories and share them with his friends. He often referred to these stories as "bawdy," though by this he did not mean stories that were smutty or blasphemous. Walter Hooper tells us that Lewis did not enjoy that kind of humor and would not disguise his annoyance when such a story was told in his presence. Instead, he liked stories that pointed out the ridiculousness inherent in situations, and loved to repeat foolish things that he might overhear. One example of the kind of "bawdy" story Lewis liked is this one that he told to Kingsley Amis and Brian Aldiss. It turns on the name of a character (Bottom) in one of Shakespeare's plays:

> *A Bishop of Exeter…was giving prizes at a girls' school. "They did a performance," said Lewis, "of A Midsummer Night's Dream, and the poor man stood up afterwards and made a speech and said (piping voice): 'I was very interested in your delightful performance, and among other things I was very interested in seeing for the first time in my life a female Bottom.'*[174]

But comedy can be more than just an entertaining adornment. It can also be an excellent tool for the proclamation of truth, especially the truth that we should not take ourselves too seriously. It can demonstrate human finitude, show our limitations and cause us to laugh at ourselves. Often laughter is the only proper response to our foolishness. As Lewis points out, even rather coarse humor can illuminate something about our human nature. These jokes can teach us one of the most important lessons of theology—that we are more than just flesh and blood machines.

> *The coarse joke proclaims that we have here an animal which finds its own animality either objectionable or funny. Unless there had been a quarrel between the spirit and the organism I do not see how this could be: it is the very mark of the two not being "at home" together.*[175]

In other words, the very fact that we find some of the functions of our body to be humorous is a good signal that we are more than just a body. We are something higher, a spiritual being, destined for eternity, but encased in a body of flesh.

Possibly Lewis' greatest achievement in humor was the satire in his book, *The Screwtape Letters*. Over and over, the messages in the book are effectively delivered by the use of satire. He gets us laughing only to make us realize that we are very often laughing at ourselves.

Of course the great danger in humor is that it might decline into mere flippancy, in which we laugh not because of the foolishness of a situation, but because we are so jaded that we laugh at everything. We live in a time when much of our humor is either sharpened with the nasty sword of personal attack or takes an ironical tone that holds nothing sacred. Screwtape advises Wormwood that this kind of humor is most effective in the battle against the Enemy (God).

> *Flippancy is the best of all...Only a clever human can make a real joke about virtue, or indeed about anything else; any of them can be trained to talk as if virtue were funny. Among flippant people the Joke is always assumed to have been made. No one actually makes it; but every serious subject is discussed in a manner which implies that they have already found a ridiculous side to it.*[176]

When we are flippant it distances us from the truth, unlike real humor which causes us to see the truth. "Humor," says Lewis, "involves a sense of proportion and a power of seeing yourself from the outside."[177] Humor helps us to realize that from God's point of view the self-important human being is a pretty funny creature! One of the powerful truths about humor is that it assumes an ideal against which we judge ourselves. If there was no ideal or expectation to fall short of, there would be nothing to laugh about. But we can laugh, and sometimes our laughter should be mixed with tears, for we still struggle to be what God would have us to be.

# TRADITION

*To study the past does indeed liberate us from the present, from the idols of our own market-place. But I think it liberates us from the past too. I think no class of men are less enslaved to the past than historians. The unhistorical are usually, without knowing it, enslaved to a fairly recent past.*[178]

*L*ewis knew that in his concern for the ideas and values of the past he was out of step with modern times. Admitting that he was something of a dinosaur, one whose belief system was almost extinct within the modern academic world, Lewis sometimes referred to himself as an "Old Western Man." He understood that the classical tradition of the west, which had bequeathed to us so many riches, was in danger of disappearing. He saw that a great rupture had taken place in our society that had put us out of touch with ancient wisdom. The cause of this rupture is an attitude he called "chronological snobbery," a prejudice against the past, based on the belief that the ever-advancing achievements of our time are making the past increasingly irrelevant.

Pointing to the triumph of technology as the primary cause of this modern temperament, Lewis noted that the progress of the machine has changed the way we perceive former times:

> *The theme [of the great changes wrought by the advent of the machine] has been celebrated until we are all sick of it, so I will here say nothing about its economic and social consequences, immeasurable though they are. What concerns us more is their psychological effect. How has it come about that we use the highly emotive word "stagnation," with all its malodorous and material overtones, for what other ages would have called "permanence"?...Why does "latest" in advertisements mean "best"?...I submit that what has imposed this climate of opinion so firmly on the human mind is a new archetypal image. It is the image of old machines being superseded by new and better ones.*[179]

Though in the world of machines we can point to a history of overcoming obstacles, of finding new and improved ways to solve problems and better our lives, this is not necessarily the case in the world of ethics, in the world of the mind and the spirit.

Lewis believed that the myth of progress was one of the most powerful motivating forces in modern society. In an essay entitled "The Funeral of a Great Myth,"[180] he suggests that the modern belief in biological evolution is often extrapolated to include constant progressive improvement in all areas of human endeavor. The result of this myth is to cause us to place great, and unwarranted, trust in our present understandings. Instead of looking to Aristotle, Aquinas or the Scriptures, we concentrate on the insights of the psychologists and the prognostications of the social science pundits. We treat the thinking of the past as irrelevant, thereby cutting ourselves off from its riches.

To believe that whatever has gone "out of date" is therefore discredited is a most arrogant and grievous error. As Lewis credits Owen Barfield with teaching him, "You must find out why it went out of date; was it ever refuted (and if so by whom, where and how conclusively) or did it merely die away as fashions do? If the latter, this tells us nothing about its truth or falsehood." If indeed, ideas simply "die away," this should serve to remind us that our own age is an historical period, just like those that have preceded it, and that it has its own "characteristic illusions." "They are," writes Lewis, "likeliest to lurk in those widespread assumptions which are so ingrained in the age that no one dares to attack or feels it necessary to defend them."[181]

This is surely one of the great values of being an attentive student of the past—it causes us to see the present more clearly. When we partake of ancient wisdom, we are given powerful insights into the inadequacies, illusions, evasions, and errors of our time. The past can provide us with a perspective from which the present can be critiqued and questioned. Lewis' attitudes toward modern times are well reflected in his own literary taste. He was a voracious reader, but his preferences tended toward the classics. It would be difficult to find anything written before the nineteenth century which he had not read. Much of the credit for Lewis' astonishing insights into modernity arise from the fact that he spent so much time at the feet of ancient thinkers, benefiting from their wisdom.

Although technology has made such tremendous leaps forward and promises to continue to overcome some of the challenges of our daily lives, there is one constant that does not change: the basic make-up of human nature. Although our environment might be different from that of a Greek citizen of Athens, a peasant farmer of ancient Palestine or a medieval monk, we share in common with them the basic traits which make up our human nature. We deal with the same desires for love, struggles with temptation, hopes for the future and awareness of our limitations.

If we have greater insight into some areas today, it is only because we are able to make use of the knowledge we have inherited from the past. As Bernardus Silvestis, a 12th century scholastic said, "We see farther because we stand on the shoulders of giants." Our debt to the past is immense. If we are willing to acknowledge it, and bend an attentive ear to what great men and women of the past have said or written, we will find that we are the heirs to a great spiritual and intellectual wealth. If we choose to ignore the wisdom of our predecessors, we will find ourselves impoverished. Perhaps Lewis' concern was prophetic, for if there was ever a time in which ancient wisdom has been so arrogantly disregarded, it is our own. Despite our technological achievements, we struggle to find a way to live our lives with dignity and humanity. Our dilemma: we can split the atom, but we cannot seem to keep our marriages from splitting.

# Common Sense

*A great many of those who 'debunk' traditional or
(as they would say) 'sentimental' values have in the
background values of their own which they believe
to be immune from the debunking process.*[182]

Lewis valued the insights of the ancient thinkers far
above those of modern philosophers, theologians and
writers. Throughout his writings you are more likely to find
references to Aristotle, Plato, Aquinas, Augustine, Johnson or
Hooker than to any modern thinkers. His attitudes were so
backward-looking that the "Society for the Prevention of
Progress" offered Lewis an honorary membership. He re-
sponded to this offer by writing, "While feeling that I was
born a member of your Society, I am nevertheless honoured
to receive the outward seal of membership. I shall hope by
continued orthodoxy and the unremitting practice of reaction,
obstruction, and stagnation to give you no reason for repent-
ing your favour."[183]

One of the reasons why Lewis had such a negative out-
look on modern intellectual trends is that they had lost

connection with what he saw as one of humanity's key tools for determining truth: common sense. Lewis followed in a grand tradition of thinkers who believed that human beings have an innate knowledge of truth. Modernism was "divorced by some madness from the *'communis sensus'* of man."[184] Such common sense is the knowledge of what is truly valuable and is not dependent upon learning or academic culture. It is a knowledge in which the uneducated farm worker might surpass the most highly educated professor. In Lewis' own words, it is "extremely doubtful whether 'culture' produces any of those qualities which will enable people to associate with one another graciously, loyally, understandingly, and with permanent delight."[185]

"The whole modern world," he writes, "ludicrously over-values books and learning and what (I loathe the word) they call 'culture.' And of course culture itself is the greatest sufferer by this error; for second things are always corrupted when they are put first."[186] What was truly important to Lewis was the development of wisdom, which is perhaps best defined by Coleridge, when he wrote that "common sense to an uncommon degree is what the world calls wisdom."[187] One of the surest reasons for Lewis' vast popular appeal was his belief that the ultimate truths of life are not hidden only in the minds of the learned, but what is really most important in life is accessible to all. He had a gift for communicating even the most complex ideas in the most homely and entertaining way possible, appealing to the common sense of the average person. As he said, "Any fool can write *learned* language. The vernacular is the real test. If you can't turn your faith into it, then you don't understand it or you don't believe it."[188]

Michael Aeschliman, speaking of Lewis' kinship to Swift, Johnson and Chesterton, states: "A premise that all of these writers shared is that there is in the world a comprehensive and comprehensible truth, one that accommodates itself to every level of intelligence and is thus available to all men."[189] Lewis sums up the content of this truth in the first chapter of *Mere Christianity*:

> *There are two points I wanted to make. First, that human beings, all over the earth, have this curious idea that they ought to behave in a certain way, and cannot really get rid of it. Secondly, that they do not in fact behave that way. They know the Law of Nature; they break it. These two facts are the foundation of all clear thinking about ourselves and the universe we live in.*[190]

Communicating what is really important, therefore, is not so much a matter of **informing** humanity as of **reminding** them of the universal moral law. This moral law is not a great hidden truth, but one that is self-evident. In *The Abolition of Man*, Lewis demonstrates how all the great world religions and philosophies are in basic agreement on the general ethical rules by which decent human life is lived. He feared that in our modern times, moral relativism had caused us to lose sight of these essential truths. As George Orwell once remarked, "We have now sunk to a depth at which restatement of the obvious is the first duty of intelligent men."

# SUBJECTIVISM AND RELATIVISM

*When men say "I ought" they certainly think they
are saying something, and something true, about the
nature of the proposed action, and not merely about
their own feelings. But if Naturalism is true, "I
ought" is the same sort of statement as "I itch" or
"I'm going to be sick.*[191]

Lewis saw that one of the greatest hurdles to finding the
truth in our modern times, was that many people don't
even believe there is any truth to be found. Increasingly, we
are told that each person must find the truth for themselves,
and that moral and religious choices are on the same order as
choosing what kind of car to drive. Subjectivism, the belief
that objective truths about values either do not exist or cannot be found, is one of the modern intellectual tendencies
which Lewis took great pains to refute, especially in his out-
standing essay, "The Poison of Subjectivism."

In the essay, Lewis points out that no major thinker previous to modern times had "ever doubted that our judgments
of value were rational judgments or that what they discovered

was objective."[192] But in our modern era, we no longer express our judgments in terms of reason, giving a rational account for why we believe what we do. Instead, it has become a matter of feelings or sentiments:

> ...*[V]alue judgments are not really judgments at all. They are sentiments, or complexes, or attitudes, produced in a community by the pressure of its environment and its traditions, and differing from one community to another. To say that a thing is good is merely to express our feeling about it.*[193]

How far this is from the classic and Biblical tradition! In former times, we believed that rational inquiry could give us an accurate picture of reality. We believed in the value of logical consistency and in the principle of non-contradiction (that a statement and its opposite could not both be true). We believed that what we counted as truly good was not the result of our whims but was a reflection of the reality of God's creation. And we believed that rationality was the tool God had given us to explore reality and to test the truth against our own subjective whims.

If, instead of this belief in rational judgements, we hold to the position of subjectivism, then there is no ultimate guideline for truth and ethics except personal preference. Ideology, too, becomes a matter of choice. Lewis reminds us that in this case there are no grounds to criticize those we disagree with or hold to be morally reprehensible. The example at hand for him was the horror of World War II. Few would hesitate to decry the Nazi ideology, but on what grounds? "Unless there is some objective standard of good, over-arching Germans, Japanese, and ourselves alike, whether any of us obey it or not, then of course the Germans are as competent to create their ideology as we are to create ours."[194]

We must also ask ourselves why traditional values should be overturned. The usual answer is that we need to replace them with a new standard. However, though many new standards have been offered by philosophers and ethicists, none is ultimately successful because none presents a viable alternative to the innate moral law which God has implanted in each person. Lewis suggests two basic difficulties in trying to find a new basis for moral values:

> *(1) The human mind has no more power of inventing a new value than of planting a new sun in the sky or a new primary colour in the spectrum.*
> *(2) Every attempt to do so consists in arbitrarily selecting some one maxim of traditional morality, isolating it from the rest and erecting it into a* "unum necessarium."[195]

Each proposed alternative is lacking, which leads him to the conclusion that:

> *We have only two alternatives. Either the maxims of traditional morality must be accepted as axioms of practical reason which neither admit nor require argument to support them and not to "see" which is to have lost human status; or else there are no values at all, what we mistook for values being 'projections' of irrational emotions.*[196]

If we find ourselves in the unenviable position of arguing over such moral givens as the evils of sexual infidelity or murder and the necessity of preserving human dignity, we come perilously close to the subhuman status which Lewis feared.

"But," the critic will no doubt respond, "has not modern social science proven that all ethics are culturally determined?" Lewis maintains that a look at the *Encyclopedia of Religion and Ethics* will lay this idea to rest, for all of the major religions throughout the world, and throughout time, show astonishing similarities in their views on basic values. True, some cultures may be partially blind to some of the values, but it is not a situation of pure chaos and relativity. In the appendix to *The Abolition of Man*, Lewis demonstrates the universality of basic human ethical values by showing their importance in many different cultural settings.

He concluded that without objective values only individual desire is left as a standard and that "good is indeed something objective, and reason the organ whereby it is apprehended."[197] In these days when it is held that the only absolute truth is that there is no absolute truth, let us hold fast to the conviction that we are not left to navigate our lives by our whims and the call of our passions. Instead, let us be confident that God has created a moral law in our hearts and a conscience that only constant misuse can dull and desensitize.

# Sᴄɪᴇɴᴛɪsᴍ ᴀɴᴅ Rᴇᴅᴜᴄᴛɪᴏɴɪsᴍ

*No philosophical theory which I have yet come across is a radical improvement on the words of Genesis, that "in the beginning God made Heaven and Earth."*[198]

If, as we saw in the last chapter, subjectivism is the first great danger to modern civilization, the second great danger lies in what Lewis called "Scientism." Scientism is the belief that science presents the prospect of unbridled progress and improvement, promising the attainment of all human possibilities. It holds that the scientific method provides the key to solving all human problems and that science is the only rational authority in matters of knowledge. Scientism has been fed by the impressive accomplishments of modern scientific research and has led many to see science as the answer to all our human questions. But Lewis distinguishes Scientism from true science, which understands its own limitations, knowing that it can only answer the question of how, not of why.

The difficulty with Scientism is two-fold. First, it causes us to lose sight of the most important human endeavors, and second, it has a tendency toward reductionism. In his valuable study, *The Restitution of Man: C. S. Lewis and the Case Against Scientism*, Michael Aeschliman differentiates between "scientia," the knowledge of the physical world available through scientific experiment, and "sapientia," the wisdom related to the search for metaphysical understanding.

> *Man, the knower pursues two related but distinct kinds of knowledge. As "homo sciens," man the knower of "scientia," he tends to matters of fact, quantity, matter, and the physical realm; as "homo sapiens," man the knower of "sapentia," he shows his interest in the qualities of meaning, purpose, value, idea, and the metaphysical realm. If we are to have truth, neither kind of knowledge can be denied or ignored…Enthusiasts of scientism fail to see that "scientia" is utterly dependent on "sapentia" for direction and meaning.*[199]

Lewis' concern is that in our enthusiasm for scientia and the modern breakthroughs in technology and scientific understanding, we ignore the important moral, ethical, human questions which arise from its use. It is not enough to understand the intricacies of the atom or the motions of the stars: we must know how to use this knowledge wisely and understand its limitations. Lewis was certainly not against science, only its misuse for self-gratifying ends. As he wrote to Arthur C. Clarke, "I agree Technology *per se* is neutral, but a race devoted to the increase of its own power by technology with a complete indifference to ethics does seem to me a cancer in the Universe."[200]

The second misuse of science is the tendency toward reductionism, the explanation of all phenomena in purely mechanistic terms. The practical result of this philosophy is to banish the reality which is perceived only by the intellect or the heart, and to posit as reality only that which is perceived directly by the senses, that which we can see, taste, touch, smell, or measure. As Lewis pointed out, there is always a tendency to reduce reality to our sensory experience because it does indeed tell us a lot about our world.

> *The critique of every experience from below, the voluntary ignoring of meaning and concentration on fact, will always have some plausibility. There will always be evidence, and every month fresh evidence, to show that religion is only psychology, justice only self-protection, politics only economics, love only lust, and thought only cerebral biochemistry.*[201]

But such reductionism only gives us a partial explanation for reality. It tells us nothing about meaning. A quote from one of the Narnian tales will illustrate the point:

> *"In our world," said Eustace, "a star is a huge ball of flaming gas."*
> *"Even in your world, my son," replied the old man, "that is not what a star is but only what it is made of."*[202]

Or this, from an essay in *The Weight of Glory*:

> *The strength of such a [materialistic] critic lies in the words "merely" or "nothing but." He sees*

> *all the facts but not the meaning. Quite truly,*
> *therefore, he claims to have seen all the facts.*
> *There is nothing else there; except the meaning.*
> *He is therefore, as regards the matter in hand,*
> *in the position of an animal. You have noticed*
> *that most dogs cannot understand pointing.*
> *You point to a bit of food on the floor: the dog,*
> *instead of looking at the floor, sniffs at your*
> *finger. A finger is a finger to him, and that is*
> *all. His world is all fact and no meaning.*[203]

Thus, the end result of reductionism is to empty everything of significance and meaning.

> *You cannot go on "explaining away" for ever:*
> *you will find that you have explained explana-*
> *tion itself away. You cannot go on "seeing*
> *through" things for ever. The whole point of*
> *seeing through something is to see something*
> *through it.*[204]

Thus reductionism is a dead end, for it even undercuts the rationality which allows us to question and reduce! You cannot prove that there is no such thing as proof, or argue that argument is purely a biological function. Ultimately, science must take its rightful place in the scheme of knowledge. "In science we are only reading the notes to a poem; in Christianity we find the poem itself."[205]

# Morality and Virtue

*Virtue is lovely, not merely obligatory; a celestial
mistress, not a categorical imperative.*[206]

It has become fashionable today for leaders and politicians to fill the air with denunciations of moral collapse and the need to return to "family values." Too often, a cursory glance at their own lives reveals that this is more rhetoric than conviction. Perhaps the problem is that we have focused too much on the idea of values to the exclusion of virtues. A "value" is an idea we hold in our head about how things should be, it is a morally neutral term which specifies a preference. "Virtue" on the the other hand, is a quality of character which leads to action. All too often, values are something we only argue about; virtue is a way of living. In all his writings, C. S. Lewis focused on moral obedience as the key to real change in character. And that change is the goal of all morality.

Sometimes we wonder why God has instituted the moral commandments. Is it because He is some sort of cosmic killjoy? "There is a story," writes Lewis, "about a schoolboy who was asked what he thought God was like. He replied that, as far as he could make out, God was 'The sort of person who is always snooping round to see if anyone is enjoying himself and then trying to stop it.'"[207] This common misperception about God and morality arises from a failure to perceive what God's purpose is in setting up moral imperatives.

God's laws are not set up merely as a test of our obedience or as a way to control us, rather they are directions for living human life to its fullest potential. When we disregard these guidelines, the result will be a diminution of our lives or character. God's "rules" exist so that the human machine can function better. "Every moral rule is there to prevent a breakdown, or a strain, or a friction in the running of that machine."[208] We might wish, at times, that the universe was other than it is and that certain actions, like an explosion of anger or sexual promiscuity, did not carry the consequences they most assuredly do. But we cannot change reality as it was created by God, merely to suit our preferences. This desire to remake the moral rules is one of the characteristics of the modern age.

> *For the wise men of old, the cardinal problem of human life was how to conform the soul to objective reality, and the solution was wisdom, self-discipline, and virtue. For the modern, the cardinal problem is how to conform reality to the wishes of man, and the solution is technique.*[209]

Our lives are a battleground for good and evil. As Lewis shows again and again, every day we are faced with small or great decisions and choices which move us in the direction of either righteousness, or depravity. Morality is not an abstract question for debate, it is the foundation for growth in character.

> *Christianity asserts that every individual*
> *human being is going to live for ever, and this*
> *must be either true or false. Now there are a*
> *good many things which would not be worth*
> *bothering about if I were going to live only sev-*
> *enty years, but which I had better bother about*
> *very seriously if I am going to live for ever.*
> *Perhaps my bad temper or my jealousy are*
> *gradually getting worse—so gradually that the*
> *increase may not be very noticeable. But it*
> *might be absolute hell in a million years: in*
> *fact, if Christianity is true, Hell is the precisely*
> *correct technical term for what it would be.*[210]

But virtue is not simply obedience to a set of rules. "Right actions done for the wrong reason do not help to build the internal quality or character called a "virtue," and it is this quality or character that really matters."[211] God wants more than slavish obedience from us, He wants to change us. "We might think that God wanted simply obedience to a set of rules: whereas He really wants people of a particular sort."[212]

Virtue is more than just the absence of vices. It is a powerful, positive force for good in our lives. As G. K. Chesterton once wrote, "Virtue is not just the absence of vices or the avoidance of moral dangers; virtue is a vivid and separate thing."[213] One of the strengths of Lewis' writings is that he gives us such an exciting picture of what goodness looks like. His fiction is filled with characters who demonstrate that being virtuous is not a weak characteristic in a personality, but rather one of strength, courage, honor, and power. Lewis gives us pictures of good which fascinate and draw us, awakening within us the hope that we too can rise above our instincts and limitations and do the right thing. Virtue is the ability and power to choose good, which arises from a transformation of our hearts and minds. If we are not virtuous people, we are controlled by the desires and tendencies of our fallen nature.

Although freedom is one of the great themes of our society, by freedom we usually mean the ability to do what we want to do. But virtue offers us a higher freedom—the freedom not to do what we know is wrong, the freedom to resist the control of our lusts and instincts and to choose to serve God and others rather than being mired in serving the self.

To begin this process, we must deal with the little details of our daily lives. Before we tackle making good decisions on the major issues of our lives, we must learn to make proper choices on the little things: I will not use this opportunity to build myself up or tear someone else down; I will choose not to be offended over what is most likely an innocent oversight; I will not explode in anger, but will wait to hear the whole story; I will not take that "second look" of lust. It is the cumulative power of making right choices, therefore, that trains us into the practice of virtue which is, of course, the practice of godliness.

# FAITH AND OBEDIENCE

*God has been waiting for the moment at which you discover that there is no question of earning a pass mark in this exam or putting Him in your debt.*[214]

*L*ewis believed that there were two senses of the word "faith." In the first sense, which he calls "Faith A," faith means an intellectual assent to a set of beliefs. In this sense, nearly everyone has some sort of faith. And for the Christian it may mean only a mental agreement with the tenets of the Christian worldview. The other usage for the word faith, "Faith B," means trust or confidence in the God whom we have come to believe in, even when our circumstances would lead us to panic or abandon our hope.

Faith A—faith as intellectual consent—is not necessarily even a religious state. Lewis quotes the apostle James, "You believe that God is one. You do well. The demons also believe and shudder." (James 2:19) All of the great philosophical arguments for God can only produce this sort of faith, while the kind of faith Lewis sees as a Christian virtue is the kind that surrenders completely to God—Faith B.

For the Christian, faith is more than a property of the intellect. Although we must begin the journey of faith by embracing some ideas about God, these are simply not sufficient in themselves. They do not change our lives or offer us salvation. Lewis knew about God and believed that He existed for some time before he finally committed himself to God as a Christian believer. We must come to see that faith is a 'gift,' not an intellectual attainment. Faith A is only the doorway through which we move into Faith B.[215]

This might lead some to conclude that faith, then, is simply a property of our emotions. Lewis would not agree. In our day, there are those who suggest that faith is an emotional state that we must stir up within ourselves. Lewis suggests that emotions really play a very minor role in true faith. Very often it means believing in spite of how we feel. God's reality and commitment to us are objective realities. We do not need to feel them to be true; they simply are true.

Ultimately, it is a matter of trust. Our faith is not in a system or a philosophy, but in a personal God. We trust "not because 'a God' exists, but because *this* God exists."[216]

> *There are things, say in learning to swim or to climb, which look dangerous and aren't. Your instructor tells you it's safe. You have good reason from past experience to trust him. Perhaps you can even see for yourself, by your own reason, that it is safe. But the crucial question is, will you be able to go on believing this when you actually see the cliff edge below you or actually feel yourself unsupported in the water? You will have no rational grounds for disbelieving. It is your senses and your imagination that are going to attack belief.*[217]

The conflict, as Lewis points out, is not so much between faith and reason as it is between faith and sight. This is exactly the conflict that is addressed in the New Testament. We are not asked to believe in spite of evidence. The character of God and the rationality of faith give us solid reasons to believe. The issue is: will we follow what we know to be true and the One we know we can depend on, or will we panic and trust only in the way the situation looks? "Our faith in Christ wavers," writes Lewis, "not so much when real arguments come against it as when it looks improbable…"[218] Growing in faith means learning to believe, even in the teeth of lust, jealousy, fear, boredom, and indifference. It is, once again, not a blind faith, but a faith in the character of the One who loves us.

> *Faith, in the sense in which I am here using the word, is the art of holding on to things your reason has once accepted, in spite of your changing moods. For moods will change, whatever view your reason takes…Now that I am a Christian I do have moods in which the whole thing looks very improbable: but when I was an atheist I had moods in which Christianity looked terribly probable…unless you teach your moods "where they can get off," you can never be either a sound Christian or even a sound atheist, but just a creature dithering to and fro, with its beliefs really dependent on the weather and the state of its digestion.*[219]

So, faith is not something we have to "work up" within ourselves. It is, instead, the settled conviction that all will be right if we continue to trust, the dawning realization that we cannot live our lives as we know we ought without help from God. It is coming to the end of our rope and realizing that it is God who holds the other end, it is surrendering and laying down our arms. It is learning that we must stop trying to please God and recognize that He is pleased with our realization that we need Him. "[I]t is not trying that is ever going to bring us home. All this trying leads up to the vital moment at which we turn to God and say, "You must do this, I can't."[220] We must reach a point at which we despair of all our efforts and realize that what we cannot do for ourselves, God will do for us.

This realization will be followed, of course, by obedience. Our surrender is little good without the intention to obey. "[I]f what you call your 'faith' in Christ does not involve taking the slightest notice of what He says, then it is not faith at all—not faith or trust in Him, but only intellectual acceptance of some theory about Him."[221]

To have the kind of faith that obeys God even when there is no attending feeling of conviction is to defuse one of the Devil's most powerful tools. As Screwtape writes to Wormwood: "Our cause is never more in danger than when a human, no longer desiring, but still intending, to do our Enemy's will, looks round upon a universe from which every trace of Him seems to have vanished, and asks why he has been forsaken, and still obeys."[222]

# EMOTIONS

*Feelings come and go, and when they come a good
use can be made of them: they cannot be our regular
spiritual diet.*[223]

Everyone likes to feel good. And when it comes to our
faith, there is something very special about the exalted
feelings which are sometimes the result of a consciousness of
God's love for us and a realization of His presence in our lives.
But C. S. Lewis learned to distrust emotions and not to look
to them to validate the truth of his faith or to assure him that
he was on the right spiritual or ethical path. "Now that I am
a Christian I do have moods in which the whole thing looks
very improbable: but when I was an atheist I had moods in
which Christianity looked terribly probable."[224]

Our feelings are so changeable, influenced by the weather
or the state of our digestion. They only register within us an
emotional response, telling us nothing about how things
really are. We must hold to what we know to be true, even
when our emotions tell us otherwise. As Lewis wrote to a
struggling correspondent: "Don't bother much about your
feelings." Our feelings are not us, he says, but only a thing

which happens in us and to us. We should be thankful when they are humble, loving, or brave, and work to alter them if they are conceited, selfish or cowardly.[225] We cannot count on our emotions to help us make the right decisions. "Our emotional reactions to our own behavior are of limited ethical significance."[226] Much of the time, to do the right thing we have to act differently than we feel.

In a letter to a brand new Christian, who had written to Lewis for counsel on how to begin to live the Christian life, he offers sage advice on religious emotions. While he does not wish to quash enthusiasm or dampen excitement over new-found feelings of joy, he does want to offer a proper caution against dependence upon emotion.

> *Accept these sensations with thankfulness as birthday cards from God, but remember that they are only greetings, not the real gift. I mean that it is not the sensations that are the real thing. The real thing is the gift of the Holy Spirit which can't usually be—perhaps not ever—experienced as a sensation or emotion. The sensations are merely the response of your nervous system. Don't depend on them. Otherwise when they go and you are once more emotionally flat…you might think that the real thing is gone too.*[227]

There is nothing wrong with emotions, but we must never begin to look to them for authentification of our faith, or wait to "feel like it" before we act as we know we should. We don't have to *feel* charitable to *act* with charity!

A very large part of growth into Christian maturity is learning to act as we know Christ would have us act, even when it runs cross-grain to our emotional tendencies. Many of us want to wait until we feel the stir of love and compassion within our hearts to show love to somebody. But Christian maturity, Christ-likeness, calls us to act in spite of our emotions. I may feel no compassion for my neighbor, but I am called to help him anyway. Day after day, our actions should proceed from what we know, not how we feel.

We need to act as Christ would have us act, even when we experience little emotional satisfaction from doing so. In a very real sense, we "dress up like Christ." Pretending to be like Him actually begins the process of changing ourselves so that we become like Him. In *Mere Christianity*, Lewis uses the example of little boys playing at war. In the process of their games, of pretending to be soldiers, they begin to develop some of the skills which real soldiers need to possess. So we too, when we do what Christ would have us do, become just a little more like Him.

Sometimes, when we are going through a difficult time in our lives, it is hard to stir ourselves to those disciplines which bring growth in our lives: prayer, church attendance, Scripture reading. But these are just the times when we most need to be faithful. We must commit ourselves to "show up," to continue to practice the disciplines of our lives, to stand firm in what we believe, even when what we feel fails to come into line with it. Moods are changeable, the truth is eternal. Lewis suggests that what proceeds from this dedication may be especially dear to God, for it rises from our will, our deepest commitment to follow Him:

> *I have a notion that what seem our worst prayers may really be, in God's eyes, our best. Those, I mean, which are least supported by devotional feeling and contend with the greatest disinclination. For these, perhaps, being nearly all will, come from a deeper level than feeling.*[228]

Perhaps it is in the area of temptation, that we most experience the need to live by faith, not by feelings. The easiest target for the Devil is our emotional life. It takes so little emotional upset to debilitate our faith. Our emotions will almost always lead us astray, for they are part of our fallen nature. We must will to do what is right if we are to defeat temptation in our lives.

In *The Screwtape Letters*, Lewis reminds us that we will experience seasons of great spiritual awareness as well as seasons of dryness and emotional desolation. These he calls "peaks" and "troughs." We should rejoice in the "peak" times but not lose heart when we find ourselves in the "troughs." The troughs are a part of the normal cycle of our spiritual lives, not a punishment or abandonment by God. If we hold fast in the dark times, we will learn the truth—that our faith does not depend upon our feelings.

# PRAYER

*For most of us the prayer in Gethsemane is the only model. Removing mountains can wait.*[229]

*A*s a young man, Lewis' struggle with prayer was one of the things that turned him against Christianity. He had experienced unanswered prayer, both when he prayed fervently for his mother's health, only to see her die, and also when he petitioned God to remove him from the boarding school he so loathed. Serious attempts at prayer became an almost intolerable burden to the young Lewis, as he worked himself into a frenzy with his efforts to concentrate and not be distracted. Experiencing constant failure, he gave up praying, and soon after, gave up his faith.

When he was converted some years later, therefore, he gave a great deal of thought to the meaning and practice of prayer. His insights on this important Christian practice show a commendable balance and wisdom. One of his last books, *Letters to Malcolm, Chiefly on Prayer*, is surely one of the modern masterpieces on the devotional life.

To anyone thinking seriously about the subject, one of the first questions we must ask ourselves is the simple inquiry, "why pray?" From one point of view, it really makes very little sense. If indeed, God is sovereign, why does He need our prayers? He knows our needs before we ask and is certainly not without the means to accomplish His will. He doesn't need to be told what is best or urged to do it. A moment's reflection, says Lewis, shows that God does not need man to accomplish anything. He could produce food without farmers, knowledge without scholars and conversions of the heathen without missionaries. And yet He chooses to use men and women for the accomplishing of His will. He makes us collaborators in His work; this is the way He chooses to execute His will. As Lewis writes in a poem:

> *No stranger that omnipotence should*
> *choose to need*
> *Small helps than great—no stranger*
> *if His action lingers*
> *Till men have prayed, and suffers*
> *their weak prayers indeed*
> *To move as very muscles*
> *His delaying fingers...* [230]

Lewis felt awe at the way God would sometimes miraculously answer prayers. Once, he felt a strong compulsion to go to the barber even though his hair did not really need cutting and he disliked getting his hair cut. His barber was a Christian brother who often sought Jack's counsel and advice. When he arrived that day, he found that the barber needed to see him and had been praying that he would come. "If I had come a day or so later I should have been of no use to him." [231] When Joy was sick and dying, Lewis asked a young minister to pray for her. Though she had been given up on by the doctors, she experienced a miraculous remission of her cancer. Jack came to know the power of answered prayer.

Of course, the conviction that God answers prayer does not mean that every prayer is answered as we would like. Unfortunately, like Lewis did as a youth, many believers hold very immature ideas about prayer. They see it as a magical way of overcoming adversity, or of getting what they want or think they need. God promises to hear our prayers, but not to grant every little whim. "I must often be glad," writes Lewis, "that certain past prayers of my own were not granted."[232] It is unrealistic to think that we will get everything we pray for because "if an infinitely wise Being listens to the requests of finite and foolish creatures, of course He will sometimes grant and sometimes refuse them."[233] Even Christ, praying in the garden of Gethsemane, did not get what He asked for in a moment of weakness. Prayer is more like a child addressing requests to a wise parent than the waving of a magic wand.

In *Letters to Malcolm*, Lewis writes to a fictitious friend that "however badly needed a good book on prayer is, I shall never try to write it…for me to offer the world instruction about prayer would be impudence."[234] Of course, he must have written that with a wry smile, because that is exactly what he does in this book. But Lewis teaches about prayer not as an expert, but as a fellow struggler.

Lewis knew that prayer was a serious activity, not something we can take lightly. It is an act that requires our fullest effort and concentration. He kept an ever-growing list of people he needed to remember in prayer, and liked to find moments of silence and solitude in which to pour out his heart to God. To make prayer a perfunctory act at the close of our day is to rob it of its meaning. "I entirely agree with you," he wrote in *Letters to Malcolm*, "that no one in his senses, if he has any power of ordering his own day, should reserve his chief prayers for bed-time—obviously the worst possible hour for any action which needs concentration."[235]

Lewis used both written and spontaneous prayers. The ready-made prayers of others could, he believed, give us perspective on our own struggles and were often based upon solid theological truths that we need to call to remembrance and confess aloud. But Lewis more frequently prayed his own spontaneous prayers, which have the advantage of being very specific about present needs and circumstances. Sometimes he would practice what he called "festooning," a combination of these two forms of prayer. He would take a prayer like the Lord's Prayer and use it, line by line, as a spur to his own prayers. Praying "Our Father," he would thank God for what this meant, then praying "lead us not into temptation," he would bring his own struggles with sin before the Father.

But how we pray is not as important as our attitude in prayer. Prayer puts us in the place of complete dependence upon God. We must be open and honest, not trying to disguise our feelings or make sure that our requests seem appropriate. Instead, we should come before God with even our most trivial concerns. "I fancy that we may sometimes be deterred from small prayers by a sense of our own dignity rather than God's."[236]

In *The Magician's Nephew*, Digory complained that Aslan had sent him and Polly on a long journey without providing them with food. Fledge, their horse, was convinced that Aslan would have provided it if they had asked. Polly demurred that Aslan would surely know that they needed food without having to be asked. The horse answered, his mouth full of grass, that though Aslan would know, he seemed to like to be asked.[237] He who loves us wants us to come to Him to get our needs met.

# SIN

*We are all fallen creatures and all very hard to
live with.*[238]

What is wrong with mankind? It is obvious to anyone
who takes even a cursory look at the state of our
world that something has gone terribly wrong with the
human race. This is quite obviously not the best of all possible worlds, despite the most optimistic hopes of crusading
politicians. Our world is morally bankrupt, and to the naked
eye evil seems triumphant.

But, as C. S. Lewis so often emphasized, the problem is
not that this is an innately evil world, but that it is a good
world gone bad. Without the doctrine of the fall of man, it is
hard to make sense of the human condition or to have any
real optimism about the future. If man is only a rational animal with uncontrollable desires, then pessimism would be the
only sane response. But, as Lewis shows us, we are more than
animals and being human is not at all a bad thing. The problem with man as he is now is that due to his fallenness, he is

not fully human because he is not now as God intended him to be. We are at present, members of a "spoiled species."

Our Fall is hidden somewhere in the mists of past history, but its effects are with us today. The temptation to be like gods is the continuing temptation we face. To reject God and be our own master is the root of most of the evil in our world. "The Fall is simply and solely Disobedience—doing what you have been told not to do: and it results from Pride—from being too big for your boots, forgetting your place, thinking that you are God."[239] Men and women have always hoped that they

> ...*could set up on their own as if they had created themselves—be their own masters—invent some sort of happiness for themselves outside of God, apart from God. And out of that hopeless attempt has come nearly all that we call human history—money, poverty, ambition, war, prostitution, classes, empires, slavery—the long terrible story of man trying to find something other than God which will make him happy.*[240]

How foolish it is to think that we are able to live our lives without God. "A creature revolting against a creator is revolting against the source of his own powers—including even his power to revolt.... It is like the scent of a flower trying to destroy the flower."[241]

> *From the moment a creature becomes aware of God as God and of itself as self, the terrible alternative of choosing God or self for the centre is opened to it. This sin is committed daily*

> *by young children and ignorant peasants as*
> *well as sophisticated persons, by solitaries no*
> *less than by those who live in society: it is the*
> *fall in every individual life, and in each day of*
> *each individual life, the basic sin behind all*
> *particular sins: at this very moment you and I*
> *are either committing it, or about to commit it*
> *or repenting it…The gravitation away from*
> *God, "the journey homeward to habitual self,"*
> *must, we think, be a product of the Fall.*[242]

Lewis felt that the present spiritual state of fallen humanity was so desperate that it would be dangerous for us to travel in space, lest we carry our spiritual infection to potentially unfallen worlds. In an essay entitled "Religion and Rocketry," Lewis paused to consider what it might be like, if in our space travels, we were to stumble upon such an unfallen race. He muses that we would probably initially feel superior to that race. We would "have a grand time jeering at, duping, and exploiting its innocence; but I doubt if our half-animal cunning would long be a match for god-like wisdom, selfless valour, and perfect unanimity."[243] In his *Space Trilogy*, Lewis explored this very possibility, reenacting the events of the Garden of Eden on an extraterrestrial stage. His conclusion is that fallen man is morally unfit to visit an inhabited world!

In *Out of the Silent Planet*, Lewis introduces a helpful word to describe the fallen state. When Ransom, the morally good scientist, is trying to enlighten the inhabitants of the planet Malachandra about the dangerous motives of his fellow space travelers, he finds that there is no word to describe their kind of evil. The best he can do is to describe them as "bent." This is a very useful term, for bent "suggests distortion, since things are not usually made bent. But it also suggests the possibility of correction, since that which is merely bent is not completely broken."[244]

Because there is the hope of reformation, repentance is the necessary attitude we must have toward our own sinfulness. "Fallen man," states Lewis, "is not simply an imperfect creature who needs improvement: he is a rebel who must lay down his arms."[245] But it is difficult to preach the need for repentance to modern men and women because they so rarely feel real guilt for transgressing against the moral law. The starting point for communicating the truth lies in trying to awaken a sense of real moral guilt.

As we try to undo the effects of the Fall on our lives, it is not so much the spectacularly wicked sins that we need to concern ourselves with. It is, more often than not, the cumulative effect of the small sins that draws us away from the Light. "Murder is no better than cards if cards can do the trick. Indeed the safest road to Hell is the gradual one—the gentle slope, soft underfoot, without sudden turnings, without milestones, without signposts."[246]

But we need not despair, even though our battle with sin seems hopeless, for God has provided forgiveness for our sins.

> *No amount of falls will really undo us if we keep on picking ourselves up each time. We shall of course be very muddy and tattered children by the time we reach home. But the bathrooms are all ready, the towels put out, and the clean clothes in the airing cupboard. The only fatal thing is to lose one's temper and give it up. It is when we notice the dirt that God is most present in us: it is the very sign of His presence.*[247]

# Hell and the Devil

*"Do you really mean at this time of day to re-intro-*
*duce our old friend the devil—hoofs and horns and*
*all?" Well, what the time of day has to do with it I*
*do not know. And I am not particular about the*
*hoofs and horns.*[248]

C. S. Lewis saw a lot of evil in his life, from the obvious
horrors created by the chilling Nazi quest for power to
the more subtle evils of academic backbiting or the self-centeredness he saw in his own heart. Since the Romantic age,
ushered in by the French philosopher Rousseau, many moderns have asserted that human beings are basically good and
that evil is largely a result of societal inequalities or ignorance. But Lewis had a much more radical and realistic
perspective on evil. He saw that even the smallest instances
of human evil are part of a cosmic struggle between good and
evil, a struggle that Lewis took very seriously.

In the preface to *The Screwtape Letters*, he wrote "There
are two equal and opposite errors into which our race can fall
about devils. One is to disbelieve in their existence. The other

is to believe, and to feel an excessive and unhealthy interest in them."[249] Many in our modern age have followed the first option. In his brilliant series of books on the concept of the devil in Western intellectual history, Jeffrey Barton Russell has shown that a belief in personified evil has been with us since the very beginning, and has only recently been cast aside by our rationalistic age.[250] Why is it that even among people who believe in the reality of God, there are so many who do not believe in the reality of Satan? It is not, Lewis says, so much the force of any reasoned argument as it is simply the belief that such an idea is out of date. "The doctrine of Satan's existence and fall is not among the things we know to be untrue: it contradicts not the facts discovered by scientists but the mere, vague 'climate of opinion' that we happen to be living in."[251]

Traditional theology teaches us that Satan rebelled against God because he would not bow the knee to God's authority. John Milton's *Paradise Lost*, one of the most influential works of Western literature, is an extended meditation on this rebellion. It is interesting to note that in modern literary criticism numerous critics have come to see Satan as the hero of the poem, a tragic rebel who battles God's tyrannical rule. Lewis penned a brilliant commentary on *Paradise Lost* in which he rejects this new interpretation and expresses clearly how Milton (and indeed Lewis) saw Satan.

> *Throughout the poem he [Satan] is engaged in sawing off the branch he is sitting on, not only in the quasi-political sense...but in a deeper sense still, since a creature revolting against a creator is revolting against the source of his own powers—including even his power to revolt.*[252]

His act of rebellion is not heroic, but rather a foolish attempt to ignore the reality of God's power and character.

> *What we see in Satan is the horrible co-existence of a subtle and incessant intellectual activity with an incapacity to understand anything.*[253]

What causes the fall of Satan is the desire to exist autonomously, apart from God. This same prideful attitude is what keeps so many people willfully ignorant of God's love for them. It is the desire to live for oneself and by oneself that is the root of human fallenness. This, of course, raises the uncomfortable question of the eternal destiny of those who choose to ignore God and live only in their self-contained existence.

In *The Problem of Pain*, Lewis argues that free will demands that there be an alternative to Heaven. He admits that, like many people, he finds the doctrine of Hell unpopular, detestable and almost intolerable. That doesn't mean, however, that he finds it false. He wishes, he says, that he could truthfully proclaim that all will be saved. But he cannot, for we are given choices and are free to choose our eternal destinies. God will not force Himself on those who choose to ignore Him.

Lewis believed that Hell is a self-chosen state. "I willingly believe that the damned are, in one sense, rebels to the end; that the doors of hell are locked on the *inside*..."[254]

> *The characteristic of lost souls is "their rejection of everything that is not simply themselves." Our imaginary egoist has tried to turn everything he meets into a province or appendage of the*

*self…He has his wish—to live wholly in the*
*self and to make the best of what he finds*
*there. And what he finds there is Hell.*[255]

Lewis cleverly illustrates this concept in his marvelous fantasy novel, *The Great Divorce*. In this novel, a bus load of the residents of Hell are taken on a trip to Heaven and are given the choice to remain there or return. Most choose to return to Hell rather than remain in Heaven, for they are so concerned with themselves that Heaven, with its focus on God and others, seems intolerable to them. In Heaven, they can no longer live only for themselves but must give up their self-concern to find eternal joy. Like them, it is our self-centeredness that cuts us off from God's blessings.

*We must picture Hell as a state where everyone*
*is perpetually concerned about his own dignity*
*and advancement, where everyone has a griev-*
*ance, and where everyone lives in the deadly*
*serious passions of envy, self-importance, and*
*resentment.*[256]

Daily we make choices which prepare us to be citizens of either the Kingdom of Heaven or the Kingdom of Hell. Our choices naturally propel us along one of these two paths. As the heavenly guide in *The Great Divorce* says:

*There are only two kinds of people in the end:*
*those who say to God, "Thy will be done," and*
*those to whom God says, "Thy will be done."*
*Without that self-choice there could be no Hell.*
*No soul that seriously and constantly desires*
*joy will ever miss it.*[257]

# PLEASURE

*We have had enough, once and for all, of
Hedonism–the gloomy philosophy which says that
Pleasure is the only good. But we have hardly yet
begun what may be called Hedonics, the science or
philosophy of Pleasure.*[258]

One of the oft-heard complaints about Christianity is
that it is puritanical and stifles the enjoyment of
human life. Critics claim that the Christian ideal is a life without pleasure, a life of ascetic self-denial that only looks toward
Heaven and depreciates the value of life on the earth below.
The way that some believers have lived and taught might
lend credence to such a criticism. There are those who are
only willing to give a grudging acceptance to any earthly pleasure, but C. S. Lewis was not among them. He wholeheartedly
championed life's pleasures and the possibility of the
Christian enjoying life to the fullest. He did not see all pleasures as the work of the devil, rather, he felt that God is the
author of all true joy and pleasure.

Lewis was most definitely not a puritan. He derived great enjoyment from lighting up his pipe or cigarette, or from draining a mug of dark English beer. Whatever some modern Christians might think of it, Lewis delighted in his chosen pleasures. But he also believed in moderation, in taking care that our pleasures do not get out of hand and become the center of our lives.

All created things, he taught, are good in themselves. They only become bad through misuse. As Screwtape counsels Wormwood, "I know we have won many a soul through pleasure. All the same it is His invention, not ours. He made the pleasures: all our research so far has not enabled us to produce one."[259] Humanity's pleasures would have, he argued, been more intense and more pleasurable if the Fall had not occurred.

> *[Our] pleasure would have been greater if we had remained in Paradise. The real trouble about fallen man is not the strength of his pleasures but the weakness of his reason: unfallen man could have enjoyed any degree of pleasure without losing sight, for a moment, of the First Good.*[260]

Lewis did not equate pleasure with sin, but that did not mean that the pursuit of pleasure could not become a sin. He warned that a great deal of mischief had been done by limiting the idea of temperance to alcohol, without realizing that intemperance is a temptation in almost every activity we undertake.

> *A man who makes his golf or his motor-bicycle the centre of his life, or a woman who devotes*

*all her thoughts to clothes or bridge or her dog,
is being just as "intemperate" as someone who
gets drunk every evening. Of course, it does not
show on the outside so easily: bridge-mania or
golf-mania do not make you fall down in the
middle of the road. But God is not deceived by
externals.*[261]

Therefore, he warned, we must not see the pleasures of
the body as the worst kind of sin, for there are warped spiritual pleasures that are much more hazardous to our spiritual
health.

*The sins of the flesh are bad, but they are the
least bad of all sins. All the worst pleasures are
purely spiritual: the pleasure of putting other
people in the wrong, of bossing and patronizing
and spoiling sport, and back-biting; the pleasures of power, of hatred. For there are two
things inside me, competing with the human
self which I must try to become. They are the
Animal self and the Diabolical self. The
Diabolical self is the worst of the two. That is
why a cold, self-righteous prig who goes regu-
larly to church may be far nearer to hell than a
prostitute.*[262]

On the other hand, pleasures can be a positive influence
in our spiritual lives as they can be an impetus for thankful-
ness. The small glimpses of eternal joy that we experience can
spur us on to worship. "I have tried," wrote Lewis, "to make
every pleasure into a channel of adoration."[263]

The real problem many of us face with pleasure is that

we allow it too high a priority in our lives. We feel that above all else, we must be happy. And there are television commercials and self-help books that emphasize its importance and tell us how we can attain it. But should we be focused on happiness as our goal? "We Have No Right To Happiness" was the title Lewis gave to the last essay he wrote before his death. It is, he says in this essay, a modern misconception that our lives should (or even can) always be happy. Too many of the circumstances which create happiness are simply beyond our control. If we make happiness the goal of our existence, we are destined to failure. "A right to happiness doesn't, for me, make much more sense than a right to be six feet tall, or to have a millionaire for your father, or to get good weather whenever you want to have a picnic."[264]

Still we tend to live our lives under the illusion that we can find things, people, and circumstances in this life which will bring us the happiness we seek. But the reason we so willingly go chasing after earthly pleasures is that we fail to really believe in the eternal pleasures that the Lord promises to us.

> *If we consider the unblushing promises of reward and the staggering nature of the rewards promised in the Gospels, it would seem that Our Lord finds our desires, not too strong, but too weak. We are half-hearted creatures, fooling about with drink and sex and ambition when infinite joy is offered us, like an ignorant child who wants to go on making mud pies in a slum because he cannot imagine what is really meant by the offer of a holiday at the sea. We are far too easily pleased.*[265]

# Art and Culture

*An author should never conceive himself as bring-*
*ing into existence beauty or wisdom which did not*
*exist before, but simply and solely as trying to*
*embody in terms of his own art some reflection of*
*eternal Beauty and Wisdom.*[266]

*A*s a young man, Lewis was an advocate of the idea
that the cultured life, that of appreciating the accomplishments of fine art, was an end in itself. In this, like many
of his generation, he followed the philosophy so well articulated by Matthew Arnold. Arnold believed that in our modern
age, since religion has been discredited and found inadequate
to the task of civilizing humanity, art could take its place.

After his conversion, Lewis admits to having continued to
hold a modified form of this view. If art could not indeed
bring salvation, it could at least be one of those things that
made life worth living. As his mind began to open to the possibility that he had overvalued art, he swung to the other
extreme and began to question whether it really had much

value at all. But, for one who made his living in the study of literature, this could hardly be a satisfactory conclusion.

Lewis knew that culture has a large influence on all of us. In fact, he admits that the sentimentality and artistic cheapness of Christian hymnody was a factor in his resistance to conversion. But that this complaint could have such importance for him that it would keep him from the Kingdom, showed him how inflated his ideas about art had become. When he looked to the New Testament he found that it seemed "if not hostile, yet unmistakably cold to culture."[267] The best we can say, he found, is that although Scripture might not discourage an appreciation for human culture, it certainly does not see it as important as we often do. For, "cultural activities do not in themselves improve our spiritual condition."[268]

But this does not mean that we should forsake culture altogether. Lewis came to the conclusion that although culture is not as important as some would have us believe, it nonetheless serves a real purpose. First, it provides us with a great deal of pleasure, and there is certainly nothing wrong with that as a motive. As he looked over his life he knew that he had experienced moments of uplifting joy and enlightenment from art, music, and literature. Second, human culture can be a source of insight into moral self-improvement and assist in the furthering of character. It is a "storehouse of the best (sub-Christian) values," useful for improving our character, even if these values fall short of the Christian ideals of virtue (the fruit of the Spirit). These values are important because even though they are not values of the spirit, they are values of the soul. And the soul cannot be neglected, for like the spirit, the soul is a creation of God.

> *Its [the soul's] values may be expected, therefore, to contain some reflection or antepast of*

> *the spiritual values. They will save no man.*
> *They resemble the regenerate life only as affec-*
> *tion resembles charity, or honour resembles*
> *virtue, or the moon the sun. But though 'like is*
> *not the same,' it is better than unlike. Imitation*
> *many pass into initiation. For some it is a good*
> *beginning.*[269]

So, Lewis concludes, art and culture have a real value to us, as long as they are kept in their proper place under the Lordship of Christ. His simple illustration is this: "I enjoyed my breakfast this morning, and I think that it was a good thing and do not think it was condemned by God. But I do not think myself a good man for enjoying it."[270]

But much of modern art and literature fails to produce even these lesser goals. Modern art has become so cryptic, so arcane, that it can only be understood by the modern critic. It's weakness is that it is removed from objective reality and situated in subjective consciousness. It is so focused on telling us about the inner life of the artist that it tells us very little about any objective reality we share with him. He is speaking a language we cannot understand.

> *It may well be that the author who claims to*
> *write neither for patron nor public but for him-*
> *self has done our art incalculable harm and*
> *bred up infinite charlatans by teaching us to*
> *emphasize the public's duty of "recognition"*
> *instead of the artist's duty to teach and*
> *delight.*[271]

This abandonment of reality arising from a haughty indifference to true communication, leads to art that is essentially lazy. "Many modern novels, poems, and pictures, which we are brow-beaten into 'appreciating,' are not good work because they are not *work* at all. They are mere puddles of spilled sensibility or reflection."[272]

On the other hand, while some are producing work that can only be appreciated by the "initiated," others are producing for popular consumption, work that is merely bad. We are left, then, with art that is merely sentimental. Because this kind of art is only used for diversion, it is tepid, trivial, marginal, habitual. It pushes our emotional buttons to evoke stock responses, but does not challenge, trouble or haunt us.

How, then, are we to approach true art, the genuine products of culture? In much the same way that the path to salvation is surrender, so the path to art appreciation is also surrender. That is "the first demand any work of art makes upon us….Look. Listen. Receive. Get yourself out of the way."[273] If we are to let art have its proper effect on us, we must expose ourselves to the very best art and culture and then let it teach us the lessons it has to offer. Though our lives are not empty without the arts, great art offers us much that will make our lives a little richer. The arts are not an end in themselves, but, as Lewis says, they can be the road to Jerusalem, a path toward the truth.

# THE LIMITS OF POLITICS

> *A sick society must think much about politics, as a*
> *sick man must think much about his digestion: to*
> *ignore the subject may be fatal cowardice for the*
> *one as for the other. But if either comes to regard it*
> *as the natural food of the mind—if either forgets*
> *that we think of such things only in order to be able*
> *to think of something else—then what was under-*
> *taken for the sake of health has become itself a new*
> *and deadly disease.*[274]

In 1951, Britain found itself in the throes of a particularly heated political struggle when the Conservative
Party, led by Winston Churchill, sought to regain the power it
had lost immediately after the Second World War. Most of the
experts expected the Conservatives to fail to recapture their
former power, but the voters proved them wrong as the
Conservative Party once again gained control of Parliament
and Winston Churchill was made Prime Minister. Weeks later,
Churchill offered C. S. Lewis the honorary title of Commander
of the British Empire, one of the most distinguished awards

that can be given to a private citizen. Although Lewis was an admirer of Churchill, he turned down the prestigious honor. His reasons reveal something powerful about Lewis' feelings about politics.

> *I feel greatly obligated to the Prime Minister, and so far as my personal feelings are concerned this honour would be highly agreeable. There are always, however, knaves who say, and fools who believe, that my religious writings are all covert anti-Leftist propaganda, and my appearance in the Honours List would of course strengthen their hands. It is therefore better that I should not appear there.*[275]

Lewis hesitated to take a place in the political spectrum, especially as his fame increased, because he did not wish his religious pronouncements to be confused with any specific political agenda.

This does not mean that he was silent about specific political issues. In various essays over the years, he discussed capital punishment, socialism, fascism, war, vivisection, conscription, crime, the welfare state, and the atomic bomb. But in his discussion of these issues, Lewis does not so much argue the merits of one particular partisan view, as look at the issues in terms of the larger underlying ethical and moral concerns they raise. Lewis held the classical view, which saw politics as serious reflection on the order and justice of society based on the moral order God ordained. He regretted the newer utilitarian style of politics that emphasized finding the most efficient means to achieve the desired end result. "How can we achieve our ends?" is the question of modern politics, rather than, as it should be, "what is just and in accord with the universal Moral Law?"

"Government," writes Lewis, "is at best a necessary evil."[276] The primary purpose of government, as he saw it, is the restraint of evil. Human nature is such that left to ourselves, we would recklessly pursue our own good to the detriment of others. Hence, Lewis believed in democracy because he felt that no one could be trusted with absolute power.

> *I am a democrat because I believe in the Fall of Man. I think most people are democrats for the opposite reason. A great deal of democratic enthusiasm descends from the ideas of people like Rousseau, who believed in democracy because they thought mankind so wise and good that everyone deserved a share in the government. The danger of defending democracy on those grounds is that they're not true...The real reason for democracy is...[that] man is so fallen that no man can be trusted with unchecked power over his fellows.*[277]

Lewis' primary concern was with the development of personal moral and spiritual responses in himself and others, not with the larger world of national and international crises. He made it a point of pride that he rarely read the newspaper. Meditating on the threat of the atomic bomb, Lewis wrote:

> *If we are all going to be destroyed by an atomic bomb, let that bomb when it comes find us doing sensible and human things—praying, working, teaching, reading, listening to music, bathing the children, playing tennis, chatting to our friends over a pint and a game of darts—*

*not huddled together like frightened sheep and*
*thinking about bombs. They may break our*
*bodies (any microbe can do that) but they need*
*not dominate our minds.*[278]

For Lewis, the ultimate things are grounded in the simplicity of daily human existence. He did not want to see politics of any sort infringing upon these primary concerns.

This does not mean, however, that his refusal to involve himself in politics expressed contentment with the present system. There was much in the contemporary world that frustrated him. He saw the faceless bureaucracy of modern Britain as a great evil. In fact, in *The Screwtape Letters* he imagines Hell itself as a kind of vast bureaucracy. He did not trust government by experts, and in *That Hideous Strength* he worries over the danger of scientists and social engineers who attempt to rule and guide society in a relativistic moral vacuum. In the same book he shows concern for the despoilation of nature in the name of progress, and frets over the dangerous allure of controlling the environment for financial gain. For fallen humanity, the temptation of power, as illustrated in many of his books, is almost irresistible, and the power of an elite usually means the alienation of the public at large.

The lure of power, which is the fundamental cause of evil in the political sphere, is ultimately a spiritual problem. That is why, unlike many modern Christians, Lewis was skeptical about how effective the Christian could be in politics without damaging the cause of the Gospel. With his eyes focused on eternal matters, he worried that over-involvement in politics could cause us to lose sight of our ultimate mission. After all, he said, "He who converts his neighbor has performed the most practical Christian political act of all."[279] If we wish to change our world for the better, we can do no better than to start in our own neighborhood.

# LOVE

*You cannot love a fellow-creature fully till you love God.*[280]

**P**robably no human experience is as surrounded by meaningless clichés as that of love. We have a generous supply of stock phrases to describe the feeling of love and its importance, but few voices offer us any real insight into this complex human experience. One of the handful of modern writers who has thought and written deeply about love is C. S. Lewis.

One of Lewis' first books was a literary study of the European courtly love tradition, *The Allegory of Love*. The insights he gained from studying the cultural development of romantic love were probably an influential factor in developing his challenge to many of our most cherished misconceptions. Late in his life he returned again to the topic, writing a careful study of love in its many forms in *The Four Loves*, a linguistic, philosophical, and theological study of the different Greek words for love.

The Greek language has four separate words to differentiate the various aspects of what we commonly call love. The first is *"storge,"* and affection is perhaps the English word that comes closest to expressing what is meant by this word. *Storge* is the love that members of a family have for one another, for example, the love of a parent for their child. It is a simple and homely kind of love, not usually made up of ecstatic emotions as much as settled peacefulness. It is a kind of love that is very important, says Lewis, because nine-tenths of the happiness we have in our lives comes from this kind of love.

The second word for love is *"philia,"* which is roughly synonymous with what we call friendship. As discussed in an earlier chapter, this kind of love was highly valued by C. S. Lewis.

The third kind of love is *"eros,"* from which we draw the English word "erotic." *Eros* is the love held between lovers, usually characterized by deep emotion and passion. Although the physical is often a part of *eros*, it should not be thought to be limited to sexual experience.

In our current cultural preoccupation with the sexual, we see *eros* gone out of control. Our single-minded obsession with sex is a sign that something serious has gone wrong with our perception of *eros*. Lewis challenges us to question our unbalanced emphasis on this area, by this humorous analogy:

> *You can get a large audience together to a strip-tease act—that is, to watch a girl undress on the stage. Now suppose you came to a country where you could fill a theatre by simply bringing in a covered plate on to the stage and then slowly lifting the cover so as to let everyone see, just before the lights went out, that it contained*

> *a mutton chop or a bit of bacon, would you*
> *not think that in that country something had*
> *gone wrong with the appetite for food?*[281]

Our sexual appetites have gone astray by overindulgence. We have elevated the sexual instinct to such a high level that it cannot bear the weight we place upon it and we end up denigrating a precious gift of God by placing too much emphasis on it.

The fourth word denotes the highest kind of love, *"agape."* "So there are 4 kinds of love, all good in their proper place, but *Agape* is the best because it is the kind God has for us and is good in all circumstances...*Agape* is all about giving, not getting.[282] *Agape* is the highest kind of love in that it can give deeper meaning to all three of the other kinds. It is a form of love that mirrors God's own love, for it is based on the idea of putting others' needs and desires before our own and about giving, rather than getting our needs met. Lewis differentiates between "gift-love" and "need-love." Gift-love asks what we can give to others; need-love asks how we can get our own personal needs met. We will never develop a mature attitude toward love as long as need is our primary motive.

*Agape* is not possible if we rely on our feelings of love. But if we act toward another as God would have us act, we will know the reality of *agape.* Especially in marriage, we must go beyond the feeling of "being in love" to the reality of acting out our love, sometimes through self-denial. Real love is not merely a feeling, but a commitment to another. "The idea that being in love is the only reason for remaining married really leaves no room for marriage as a contract or promise at all."[283] We must beware of the false siren song of our culture in the area of love.

*When we meet someone beautiful and clever*
*and sympathetic, of course we ought, in one*
*sense, to admire and love these good qualities.*
*But is it not very largely in our own choice*
*whether this love shall, or shall not, turn into*
*what we call "being in love?" No doubt, if our*
*minds are full of novels and plays and senti-*
*mental songs, and our bodies full of alcohol,*
*we shall turn any love we feel into that kind of*
*love* [284]

Love is not a state of the feelings, but of the will. "The rule for all of us is perfectly simple. Do not waste time bothering whether you love your neighbor; act as if you did. As soon as we do this we find out one of the great secrets. When you are behaving as if you loved someone, you will presently come to love him." [285]

Love can be a spiritual danger when we become so preoccupied with the beloved that we are drawn away from important spiritual realities. In its proper place, however, love can be a ladder to climb to higher spiritual understanding and experience. "All natural affections...can become rivals to spiritual love: but they can also be preparatory imitations of it, training (so to speak) of the spiritual muscles which Grace may later put to a higher service..." [286]

Conversely, when our love for God is the deepest and central love in our lives, it can enrich and strengthen all the loves on every other level, because God Himself is the source of love. "When I have learnt to love God better than my earthly dearest, I shall love my earthly dearest better than I do now." [287] Ultimately, our love for God is based on His love for us, and His love is not based on our merit, performance or worthiness, but upon His nature. "Christ did not die for men because they were intrinsically worth dying for, but because He is intrinsically love, and therefore loves infinitely." [288]

# PRIDE AND HUMILITY

*"Aslan," said Bree in a shaken voice, "I'm afraid I
must be rather a fool."*

*"Happy the horse [said Aslan] who knows that while
he is still young. Or the human either."* [289]

Lewis believed that pride is the mother of all sins. But if
you polled a random group of people and asked them
what was the worst of all sins, pride would certainly be low
on the list, if it even made the list at all. We moderns, and the
ancients as well, are more likely to see pride as a virtue than
as a vice. To be independent and self-sufficient are qualities
that we admire greatly. And though there is a good aspect to
these traits, they can very easily find their source in the most
deadly of sins: pride.

Pride, at its root, is self-centeredness. It is the desire that
everything and everyone revolve around our own perceived
needs and wants, the refusal to see things through the eyes of
others. Pride is not one of the sins that comes from our animal nature, but is a purely spiritual sin, birthed in Hell itself.

It is the sin that made Satan who he is, for he refused to bow to God's rightful authority as Creator. When we are proud, we cut ourselves off from God and from others.

> *It is pride which has been the chief cause of misery in every nation and every family since the world began. Other vices may sometimes bring people together: you may find good fellowship and jokes and friendliness among drunken people and unchaste people. But pride always means enmity—it is enmity. And not only enmity between man and man, but enmity to God.*[290]

Pride is a vice we overlook in ourselves, but despise when we see it in others. "There is one vice of which no man in the world is free; which everyone in the world loathes when he sees it in someone else; and of which hardly any people, except Christians, ever imagine that they are guilty themselves."[291]

One of the reasons we are not as severe with pride as we should be is that we don't have a very clear idea of its opposite: humility. Because we see humility as weakness, we do not value it as highly as we ought.

> *Do not imagine that if you meet a really humble man he will be what most people call "humble" nowadays: he will not be a sort of greasy, smarmy person, who is always telling you that, of course, he is nobody. Probably all you will think about him is that he seemed a*

> *cheerful, intelligent chap who took a real inter-*
> *est in what you said to him… he will not be*
> *thinking about humility: he will not be think-*
> *ing about himself at all.*[292]

Everyone struggles against pride. The habit of thinking of ourselves above everything else seems to be a common trait of human nature. In a letter to Arthur Greeves, Lewis wrote of an experiment he carried out to make himself aware of his own prideful thoughts. The result was a realization of how ingrown the tendency to self-centeredness really is.

> *I have found out ludicrous and terrible things*
> *about my own character. Sitting by, watching*
> *the rising thoughts to break their necks as they*
> *pop up, one learns to know the sort of thoughts*
> *that do come. And, will you believe it, one out*
> *of every three is a thought of self-admiration:*
> *when everything else fails, having had its neck*
> *broken, up comes the thought, "What an*
> *admirable fellow I am to have broken their*
> *necks!" I catch myself posturing before the mir-*
> *ror, so to speak, all day long. I pretend I am*
> *carefully thinking out what to say to the next*
> *pupil (for his good, of course) and then sud-*
> *denly I am really thinking how frightfully*
> *clever I'm going to be and how he will admire*
> *me…when you force yourself to stop it, you*
> *admire yourself for doing that.*[293]

This letter was written before he became a Christian. He soon learned that being a believer did not reduce the struggle to overcome pride. In fact, it added a new temptation:

spiritual pride. "No sooner do we believe that God loves us than there is the impulse to believe that He does so, not because He is Love, but because we are intrinsically lovable." [294]

We must especially beware of pride raising its ugly head in our religious life, causing us to become self-righteous, feeling that we are morally and spiritually superior to others. The fact is, the devil will be most pleased to let us break free from a small sin or compulsion, if only it causes us to take pride in our achievement. "The devil loves "curing" a small fault by giving you a great one." [295]

The first step to becoming humble is to realize that you are proud. Until we realize the depth of our self-conceit, we close ourselves off from the only one who can heal us of this heinous sin. We must become honest with ourselves and honest with others.

We cannot strive to be humble. "A man is never so proud as when striking an attitude of humility." [296] Instead, we must be aware of our propensity for pride and decide that we will reject it whenever we become aware of it. As long as we are aware of it in our lives we are on the right path. As Lewis writes in a letter, "Yes, pride is a perpetual nagging temptation. Keep on knocking it on the head, but don't be too worried about it. As long as one knows one is proud one is safe from the worst form of pride." [297]

# CELEBRATING THE ORDINARY

*Any patch of sunlight in a wood will show you*
*something about the sun which you could never get*
*from reading books on astronomy. These pure and*
*spontaneous pleasures are "patches of Godlight" in*
*the woods of our experience.*[298]

*I*n *Letters to Malcolm*, Lewis writes of the way that we can realize God in the ordinary experiences of our daily lives by using the phrase "patches of Godlight." All kinds of simple experiences can awaken within us a sense of God's reality, whether it be the call of a bird, the crisp sweetness of an apple or a refreshing splash in cool water. As our "mind runs back up the sunbeam to the sun," so these "patches of Godlight" give us a "tiny theophany," a vision of God.[299]

Lewis rejoiced in the simple things of life. Throughout his books he often uses such words as "homely," "domestic," "ordinary," and "simple" as positive terms of description. He was convinced that we are not limited to finding God in the highly exalted, ecstatic moments, but that His glory can also be glimpsed in the ordinary things that surround us. In an excellent essay, Ian Boyd refers to this as Lewis' "sacramental mysticism" and points to George MacDonald and G. K. Chesterton as important precursors to this view of life.[300]

The delight which Lewis found in the ordinary developed largely out of his relationship with Arthur Greeves. In a series of letters between 1914 and 1917, the two young men discuss the concept of "homeliness," a quality that Greeves celebrates, but which Lewis only comes slowly to fully appreciate. Early in the series of letters, a rather snobbish young Lewis criticizes Greeves for spending too much time reading the novels of George Eliot and Jane Austen, warning that they will give him "a very stodgy mind."[301] By the following year, after having tried some of these authors for himself, Lewis can be found praising the very quality of stodginess. Later, reflecting on how Arthur taught him to love the works of Dickens and Austen, Lewis writes:

> *What I would have called their "stodginess" or "ordinariness" he called "Homeliness"–a key word in his imagination. He did not mean merely Domesticity, though that came into it. He meant the rooted quality which attaches them to all our simple experiences, to weather, food, the family, the neighborhood...This love of the "Homely" was not confined to literature; he looked for it in out-of-door scenes as well and taught me to do the same.*[302]

Before he was a Christian, Lewis took a great deal of joy in simple vistas of nature and the homely things of life, but it was not until he became a believer that he discovered the "secret doctrine" that God's light is hidden in the most ordinary of objects.

Although Lewis tried to find an appreciation for the Creator in every living thing, he did not always find it. But he writes, "If I could always be what I aim at being, no pleasure would be too ordinary or too usual for such reception; from the first taste of the air when I look out of the window—one's whole cheek becomes a sort of palate—down to one's soft slippers at bed-time." [303]

George Sayer remembers the joy that Lewis received from "homely" scenes in novels, and his delight, for example, in the first sentences of Charlotte Yonge's *The Trial*, which began, "Richard? That's right! Here's a tea-cup waiting for you." [304] Though many of the best things in life arose from the cozy joys of a simple domestic life, nature was also a source of comfort for Lewis. He could find great delight in a tramp through the woods, a long walk across a field, the smell of a handful of dirt, or a moment of silent reflection by a small stream. All these things, in their own way, spoke to him of the glory of the God who revealed Himself in the small things.

Our surroundings do not have to be either romantic or rural for us to appreciate the beauty and glory in the small things. In an essay titled "Hedonics," Lewis enthuses over the unexpected joys he encounters on a train trip from Paddington Station to Harrow, through the suburbs of London:

> *It was early evening when my journey began. The train was full, but not yet uncomfortably full, of people going home...If any one had asked me whether I supposed them to be specially good people or specially happy or specially clever, I should have replied with a perfectly truthful No. I knew quite well that perhaps not ten per cent of the homes they were returning to would be free, even for that one*

> night, from ill temper, jealousy, weariness, sor-
> row or anxiety, and yet–I could not help it–the
> clicking of all those garden gates, the opening
> of all those front doors, the unanalysable home
> smell in all those little halls, the hanging up of
> all those hats, came over my imagination with
> all the caress of a half-remembered bit of
> music. There is an extraordinary charm in
> other people's domesticities. Every lighted
> house, seen from the road, is magical: every
> pram or lawn-mower in someone else's garden:
> all smells or stirs of cookery from the windows
> of alien kitchens.[305]

The peace and joy available to us in these moments of the quiet acceptance of life can tell us something about God which is unattainable in any other manner.

There are particular aspects of His love and joy which can be communicated to a created being only by sensuous experience. Something of God which the Seraphim can never quite understand flows into us from the blue of the sky, the taste of honey, the delicious embrace of water whether hot or cold, and even from sleep itself.[306]

# Transformation

*[He who will] in the long run be satisfied with nothing less than absolute perfection, will also be delighted with the first feeble, stumbling effort you make tomorrow to do the simplest duty.*[307]

God is not satisfied simply to save us, to transfer us from the ledgers of unbelief to the Kingdom of Heaven. He also wants to change us, to make real in us the righteousness that we have in Jesus Christ. We cannot do it without Him, but it does require our co-operation. Lewis points out the fact that the only path to real change in our lives is through obedience. It begins with the small things:

*Good and evil both increase at compound interest. That is why the little decisions you and I make every day are of such infinite importance. The smallest good act today is the capture of a strategic point from which, a few months later, you may be able to go on to*

*victories you never dreamed of. An apparently
trivial indulgence in lust or anger today is the
loss of a ridge or a bridgehead from which the
enemy may launch an attack otherwise impossible.*[308]

To begin to obey means to choose to live by what we
know God expects of us rather than to wait until we feel like
doing the right thing. We must, says Lewis, "pretend" to be
like Christ if we are ever to really be like Him. Lewis is not
calling for the kind of charade that is pretense, of trying to
pull the wool over on others, to convince them that you are
something you are not. Rather, it is the kind of pretending
where we act in spite of our feelings in the hope that the feelings will eventually come around. And even if they don't, the
process of transformation begins in us.

*Very often the only way to get a quality in real-
ity is to start behaving as if you had it already.
That is why children's games are so important.
They are always pretending to be grown-ups—
playing soldiers, playing shop. But all the time,
they are hardening their muscles and strength-
ening their wits, so that the pretense of being
grown-up helps them to grow up in earnest.*[309]

Lewis reminds us of the fairy tale of the very ugly man
who wore a mask of great beauty for many years and when
he finally removed it, his face had become conformed to the
mask. He who was once ugly had now taken upon himself the
beauty of the mask. The disguise had become a reality. So by
acting like Christ, through acts of obedience, we begin to
really become more like Him in our character.

But this process is not always easy. It usually demands great patience, much sacrifice, and daily vigilance. Sometimes the process of change can prove most uncomfortable, producing suffering and tears because our sins are so deeply embedded in our lives. But is it not worth the pain to have our old self removed and be made into the new creation God desires us to be? In *The Voyage of the Dawn Treader*, Lewis provides an example of this in Eustace, a thoroughly selfish and unpleasant little boy whose selfishness and thoughtlessness caused him to be turned into a dragon.

> *He had turned into a dragon while he was asleep. Sleeping on a dragon's hoard with greedy dragonish thoughts in his heart, he had become a dragon himself…he realized he was a monster cut off from the whole human race. An appalling loneliness came over him. He began to see the others had not really been fiends at all. He began to wonder if he himself had been such a nice person as he had always supposed…When he thought of this the poor dragon that had been Eustace lifted up his voice and wept.*

Eventually there had to be a shedding of the dragon skin to find the real Eustace underneath. He began to attempt to peel back the skin and was able to remove a layer, only to find another layer underneath. Beneath that was yet another layer. He soon despaired that he could not remove all the layers by himself. Only Aslan, the Great Lion, could completely remove the skin and only by using his fearsome claws. Eustace recounts the terrible, but necessary experience:

*The very first tear he made was so deep that I*
*thought it had gone right into my heart. And*
*when he began pulling the skin off, it hurt*
*worse than anything I've ever felt...there it was*
*lying on the grass; only ever so much thicker*
*and darker and more knobbly than the others*
*had been. And there was I as smooth and soft*
*as a peeling switch and smaller than I had*
*been. Then he caught hold of me–I didn't like*
*that much I was very tender underneath now*
*that I had no skin on–and threw me in the*
*water. It smarted like anything but only for a*
*moment. After that it became perfectly delicious*
*and as soon as I started swimming and splash-*
*ing I found that all the pain had gone.*[310]

Sometimes the pain of transformation can be intense
enough that we begin to question whether it is really worth
it. But it is, for God has great things in store for His
children. We are often, Lewis points out, like the boy who fears to tell
his mother that he has a toothache, because he is afraid that
she will send him to the dentist. And the problem with the
dentist is that he will not be satisfied with merely ending our
pain. He will want to make our teeth right, and may uncover
problems other than the toothache we bring to him. God is
like that dentist.

*Dozens of people go to Him to be cured of*
*some particular sin which they are ashamed of*
*(like masturbation or physical cowardice) or*
*which is obviously spoiling daily life (like bad*

> *temper or drunkenness). Well, He will cure it all*
> *right: but He will not stop there. That may be*
> *all you asked; but if once you call Him in, He*
> *will give you the full treatment.*[311]

He didn't come to change us into nice people, but new people. He is the painter and we are the painting. He is the inventor, we are only the invention. He knows what we can be and has given His Son to make our transformation possible. His goal for us is higher than we can imagine for ourselves. "You thought you were going to be made into a decent little cottage: but He is building a palace. He intends to come and live in it Himself." [312]

# DEATH

*There are, aren't there, only three things we can do
about death: to desire it, to fear it, or to ignore it.*[313]

**D**eath is the one experience that will be shared in common by every person. No one escapes the hand of death; it is a fact of life. Every moment we live, the sand in the hourglass of our existence continues to flow, bringing our final end ever nearer. Despite its reality, death is, for many people, a forbidden subject. We can try to evade it by ignoring it. But C. S. Lewis did not. Like his literary mentor, George MacDonald, Lewis both thought and wrote a great deal about death, meditating upon its meaning for our lives.

In his book, *Miracles*, Lewis describes the two most common responses to death. The first is the stoical attitude that death "doesn't matter," that it is an unavoidable part of the life process and should be calmly accepted as such. But, as Lewis discovered after Joy's death, if death doesn't matter, then neither does birth. If death is the end, then the temporality of our human existence is the deepest truth. There is no meaning to our short-lived lives other than what we can generate for ourselves. The second major response is to consider death as our enemy, the greatest of evils. If we have no hope of eternal existence, then what could be a greater catastrophe than for our lives to end. In this view, death is the final affront to human dignity.

But Lewis found neither of these views acceptable. Instead, he suggests that death is a paradox. It is both man's deepest fear and his greatest hope. It is the thing Christ came to conquer, but it was also the necessary means through which He obtained our salvation. Death is the result of human sin, but now Christ will redeem us from it by recalling us from the grave and giving us a new celestial body. As believers, "we hope most of death; yet nothing will reconcile us to—well, its *unnaturalness*. We know that we were not made for it; we know how it crept into our destiny as an intruder; and we know Who has defeated it."[314] Because death has been defeated, we need not fear it. In his science fiction novel, *Out of the Silent Planet*, Lewis imagines a planet with an unfallen race who only knows death as a natural transition from life. Death does not bear the taint of sin.

> *The weakest of my people does not fear death.*
> *It is the Bent One [Satan], the Lord of your*
> *world, who wastes your lives and befouls them*
> *with flying from what you know will overtake*
> *you in the end. If you were subjects of Maledil*
> *[God] you would have peace.*[315]

How different this is from fallen man who dreads death so vigorously.

Lewis knew the pain of death, of losing loved ones. When he was only a child, his mother wasted away and expired, leaving him in the comfortless hands of his father, a man too deeply mired in his own bereavement to reach out to his sons. As a young man, he experienced the horror of death on the battlefield, of seeing young men fall in battle, part of the horrible toll of the First World War. Later, Lewis watched his father die and dealt with the regrets of a relationship that had never fully healed. The unexpected death of his very dear friend, Charles Williams, was a numbing loss which reminded him of his own mortality. And, of course, the death of his beloved wife, Joy, left an emptiness that was not easily filled.

One who had experienced so much death might be expected to be uncomfortable with the subject, or to be filled with bitterness over the vagaries of life. But Lewis did not see death as an enemy to be evaded at all costs. Instead, he saw in death a doorway to eternity and the promise of transformation into a "son of God."

Death then, is not the end, it is just a step on our passage to Glory. The process of death and resurrection is the way that God works to purify us, to cleanse us, to make us new. "Nothing, not even the best and noblest, can go on as it now is. Nothing, not even what is lowest and most bestial, will not be raised again if it submits to death. It is sown a natural body, it is raised a spiritual body." [316]

The process of dying begins now, by learning to die to ourselves, our desires, our self-centeredness, our sense of autonomy before God. Hence, the advice found in *Till We Have Faces*: "Die before you die. There is no chance after." [317] The beginning that God made in our salvation will be concluded when He transforms us into the image of Christ. Because of this hope, death need not be stoically rejected, heedlessly ignored, or feared.

In light of Joy's death and his own struggles to accept it, Lewis would never minimize our sorrow at the loss of a loved one. But he did not fear his own passage into eternity. Just five months before his own death, he wrote to an American correspondent about his thoughts on dying. It is a message of great hope, confidence and promise.

> *Think of yourself just as a seed patiently waiting in the earth; waiting to come up a flower in the Gardener's good time, up into the real world, the real waking. I suppose our whole present life, looked back on from there, will seem only a drowsy half-waking. We are here in the land of dreams. But cock-crow is coming. It is nearer now than when I began this letter.*[318]

# HEAVEN

*The further up and the further in you go, the
bigger everything gets. The inside is larger than
the outside.*[319]

Whenever C. S. Lewis referred to Heaven, it was usually in capital letters, for Heaven, for him, was not
just a state of mind or a symbol, but an actual place. Heaven
is the hope that gives meaning to life, the promise that God
is not yet finished with His creation. Yet many believers give
little thought to the reality of Heaven.

Lewis proposes that there are two mistakes people commonly make which lead them away from concerning
themselves with Heaven. First, some have suggested that concentrating on Heaven is a kind of escapism, an ignoring of
reality that makes us useless in the earthly realm. There is an
old phrase, "so Heavenly minded that you are no earthly
good." As Lewis states in *Mere Christianity*, this is exactly the
opposite of what is the case. "The Christians who did most for
the present world were just those who thought most of the

next." He points to the Apostles who converted the Roman Empire, the creative geniuses of the Middle Ages, and the English Evangelicals who abolished the slave trade. Their focus on the next world in fact made them more effective in this one. "Aim at Heaven," he advises, "and you will get earth 'thrown in'; aim at earth and you will get neither." [320]

The other mistake that causes people to reject the reality of Heaven is our sometimes quaint conceptions of what Heaven is: a place where angels play harps and believers wear crowns. Some respond that playing a harp forever is not their idea of how they want to spend eternity. Of course, says Lewis, we don't want to over-literalize the Biblical descriptions. These symbols refer to truths about Heaven (majesty, timelessness, ecstasy and splendor) that are far richer than literalism. The truth is, we don't know exactly what God has in store for us, but we do know it will be glorious. All we possess now are hints and guesses about that glory:

> *For if we take the imagery of Scripture seriously…then we may surmise that both the ancient myths and the modern poetry, so false as history, may be very near the truth as prophecy. At present we are on the outside of the world, the wrong side of the door. We discern the freshness and purity of morning, but they do not make us fresh and pure. We cannot mingle with the splendours we see. But all the leaves of the New Testament are rustling with the rumour that it will not always be so. Some day, God willing, we shall get in.* [321]

But, for Lewis himself, a hope in the afterlife was not a primary factor in his conversion. Lewis came to belief not on the strength of threats and promises, but because of a conviction of the truth and a desire to please God. Incredibly, it was nearly a year after his conversion before he really came to believe in a life after death. Because his conviction came as the result of careful thinking, Heaven is a major theme in many of his books. In his fiction he has put flesh on his concepts, particularly in *Perelandra, The Voyage of the Dawn Treader* and *The Last Battle*, but most especially in *The Great Divorce*, a book whose action mostly takes place in Heaven. He gives us pictures that set us longing for eternity.

Lewis sometimes referred to this present world as the "shadowlands." His belief in Heaven was so strong that this world only seemed to him to be a shadow of the next. This conviction did not mean that he thought this world unimportant; only that he cherished the promise that one day we would be with God and know as we are known. The greatest of human events pales in comparison with that promise.

One of the greatest glories of Heaven will be to see what God will make of us. As we give ourselves to God, we begin to truly become ourselves. But this is only the beginning of a process that will culminate in Heaven. God has a plan for us, something He wants to make of us, that only awaits eternity for fruition.

> *Your soul has a curious shape because it is a hollow made to fit a particular swelling in the infinite contours of the divine substance, or a key to unlock one of the doors in the house with many mansions. For it is not humanity in the abstract that is to be saved, but you - you the individual reader...Blessed and fortunate creature, your eyes shall behold Him and not another's. All that you are, sins apart, is des-*

*tined, if you let God have His good way, to
utter satisfaction....Your place in Heaven will
seem to be made for you and you alone,
because you were made for it.*[322]

Because of his hope in Heaven, Lewis had little fear of
death. He desired the fulfillment of the longing which had
haunted him all his life. That longing could only be filled by
eternity with God, when what we have been searching for all
our lives will be within our reach. The Narnian tales end with
the death of the children in a railway accident. Lewis writes:

*The term is over: the holidays have begun. The
dream is ended: this is the morning...All their
life in this world and all their adventures in
Narnia had only been the cover and the title
page: now at last they were beginning Chapter
One of the Great Story, which no one on earth
has read: which goes on for ever: in which every
chapter is better than the one before.*[323]

# C. S. Lewis:
# His Legacy

# THE LEWIS PHENOMENON

*W*hen we think of leaders, we usually think of those who blaze new political trails, those who by their actions and their rhetoric draw masses of people to a new vision of society, or who make radical innovations that bring new security or strength to a people. To include Lewis in a series of books on great leaders might therefore seem, at first blush, an unusual choice. He never sought for or held any political office and made very few explicit public statements about political policy. His public speaking, though effective, was not extensive. But Lewis truly was a leader in the sphere of culture. He shaped the thoughts, and thereby the actions, of countless people in his own time and afterward, mostly through the quiet influence of his books.

What is it that makes the books of an Oxford and Cambridge professor who died over 30 years ago continue to be so popular today? Why is his influence still so strongly felt, that he is one of the most-quoted of religious authors? Why is it that two of his books[324] still rank among the bestselling Christian books month after month and that his children's books have achieved classic status? What has kept nearly all his books in print, including some rather specialized literary titles? Why is the late in life romance of a confirmed bachelor so interesting that it has spawned two films, a Broadway play, and at least three books? And how did this unassuming English professor come to be seen as a major cultural force for modern Christians? What is it that makes Lewis' books so enduring?

It seems to me that the factors behind what we might justifiably call "the Lewis phenomenon" are three-fold. Lewis combined three qualities in his writing and in his personal life which have worked together to make him one of the great Christian communicators of the twentieth century. First, he emphasized the reasonableness of the Christian gospel, showing that it was based on logic and common sense, not upon wishful thinking. Second, he used his incomparable imagination to reclothe the truth of the gospel in a fresh and sometimes surprising garb, which allowed it to speak afresh to contemporary men and women. Third, he demonstrated in both his writing and his personal life that the gospel was existentially viable, that it was a truth we could live out in practical ways, manifesting a reflection of God's own holiness. These factors combine in such a way to demonstrate that they are not exclusively separate characteristics, but that reason, imagination, and holiness can form an integrated whole.

# REASON

*F*or people of his own time, and countless readers since, Lewis has provided a confirmation of the intellectual validity of the Christian faith, that it is a belief system which "makes sense." Lewis saw that truth was not merely a matter of subjective opinion, but an objective reality that could be grasped by the human mind. He believed that, in the arena of faith, we are not left to rely on changeable human emotions or dark guesses about the nature of reality. For God has given us a resource through which we can attain to truth: the mind. Because of this emphasis, Lewis' writings have been a lifeline of sanity and respectability to believers who want intelligent answers to life's perplexing questions. In our day, Lewis continues to be a major source of inspiration for those raised in a Christian environment that emphasizes the emotional comforts of faith but tends to neglect its intellectual substance and implications. For those taught that Christianity is mainly a matter of the heart, Lewis shows that we don't have to disengage our rational faculties to enter into the life of faith.

Lewis' writings have the quality of appealing to strong logical argument as well as to our basic common sense. Many who would want to believe find themselves with a number of rational hurdles they must get over to accept a posture of faith. They cannot simply dismiss their questions as irrelevant or unimportant. One who wants to believe with their whole heart must first convince themselves that the Christian story is the truth. Lewis never swept aside the intellectual hurdles, saying that such questions do not matter. Instead, he showed the way over them by demonstrating that Christian orthodoxy was not irrational or foolish, but rather, that it was the most intellectually compelling answer to human dilemmas. While the truths of faith may not be empirically provable, they are certainly not irrational or nonsensical. Lewis provided us with a living example of intellectual boldness that does not have to back down in the face of highbrow attack. In his autobiography, *Born Again*, Charles Colson tells of how deeply the book *Mere Christianity* affected him. He is typical of many individuals for whom Lewis' books played a major role in preparing them to accept the gospel of Christ.

Lewis' strength is that even when talking about the most complex ideas, he finds ways to bring them alive to us. He discovers simple analogies, hidden in the normal activities of our lives, which help us relate to the profoundest truths. At the same time he never talks down to his readers but appeals to our reason and good sense. He lifts the common reader up to his level in the most painless manner, using abundant humor and wry self-deprecation. But in the end, he always calls us to think for ourselves and suggests the most reasonable conclusion.

In a day of emotional appeals and the confusion of the gospel with political agendas, Lewis is a refreshing voice to assure us that we need not jettison our intellect to believe. Instead, we may take confidence in the fact that Christianity makes good logical sense. It is not just a belief, one of many equal options—it is the truth.

# IMAGINATION

If Lewis' only accomplishment had been to present the Christian worldview in an intellectually compelling manner, there would be little to distinguish him from any number of Christian philosophers and theologians who have emphasized the rational element of the gospel. What sets Lewis apart from them, and allows him to speak so effectively to so many varied people, is his ability to communicate in a way that is creatively compelling as well as intellectually satisfying. Lewis demonstrates the power of an imagination which has been captured for the cause of truth.

He showed us that the proclamation of the gospel does not have to be didactic and doctrinaire. Lewis' flights of fantasy and creativity give us new eyes to see the "old old story." He follows the example of Jesus, who was Himself a storyteller. The majority of Jesus' teaching ministry was given to the telling of parables, anecdotes and illustrations, not to the dry unfolding of doctrine. Jesus knew that by capturing the imagination you could capture the heart. Sometimes we have become so jaded to the truth that only a story can cause us to really see. Whereas a confrontational statement can be easily rejected by the hearer, a story has the ability to sneak up upon a person, moving them at the deepest level and preparing them to see the truth from a new perspective.

In Lewis' work the gospel is embodied in story, in myths, in analogies and allegories in order that we may see it afresh. If we take a moment to consider it, we will realize that all our thinking is done in images. Even our most abstract language cannot help but partake of images that turn our abstract ideas into word pictures that we use for holding the idea in our head. We cannot, for example, speak of the glory of God without holding some sort of picture in our mind of what glory looks like. So Lewis has, throughout his books, provided us with many memorable pictures that give flesh to our theological abstractions. How many, for example, have been given new glimpses into God's actions and character through *The Chronicles of Narnia* or understood more clearly the wiles of the devil through the witty letters of Screwtape to Wormwood. Although Lewis gave us many riches in his rational arguments, surely his most enduring literary legacy is in his creative writing.

# HOLINESS

*T*here is, as well, a sense of holiness which pervades most of Lewis' work, a sense that through the doorway of his prose we have stepped from our world into another realm, a realm suffused with a holy light. Like no other writer who comes to mind, he gives us a picture of Heaven that draws us, that sets off a longing in our hearts, that awakens a desire for eternity. Lewis once wrote that it was the sense of holiness which drew him to the books of George MacDonald. It is surely this, within Lewis, that continues to draw people to his writings: not only intelligence and vivid imagining, but also holiness. He helps us to see a reality beyond that of our own experience.

Lewis demonstrates in his books the positive, attractive power of good. Many novelists and storytellers find it much easier to create interesting evil characters than good ones. Even such a master as Milton, in his *Paradise Lost*, has created, in Satan, a character that is far more convincing, interesting and compelling than the character of God. Satan is vivid and memorable, but God is rather stuffy and forgettable. Lewis had a very sensible explanation for why this was so:

> *To make a character worse than oneself it is*
> *only necessary to release imaginatively from*
> *control some of the bad passions which, in real*
> *life, are always straining at the leash; the*
> *Satan, the Iago, the Becky Sharp, within each of*
> *us, is always there and only too ready, the*
> *moment the leash is slipped, to come out and*
> *have in our books that holiday we try to deny*
> *them in life.*[325]

Of course we know that Lewis is correct in this assessment. That is what makes his own strength at picturing true goodness so awe inspiring. Over and over in his fiction he gives us convincing pictures of goodness, helping us to believe in both its possibility and reality. He shows us that true goodness is much more powerful, inviting and strong than evil, which is only a pale shadow. The characters that fix in our minds from Lewis' books are the good ones.

Such a picture of holiness could be very discouraging to us, mired as we are in our sinful nature, except for the fact that Lewis is very practical in his approach to the possibility of the transformation of our character. Though his writings are distinguished by their intelligence and creativity, they are also distinguished by their practicality. Lewis does not write abstract theological tomes or philosophize about arcane issues. His wide-ranging knowledge and immense wisdom are focused on the task of showing us how to live out the teachings of the gospel. There is always a sense of measured words, careful thought, achievable actions. He shows us the steps by which the Christian vision can be lived out in the rough and tumble of our daily lives. In Lewis' books, goodness seems attainable.

He is realistic about the imperfections of human nature,

always aware of how far both he and we will fall short. Often, before calling us to a high goal, he admits how far he himself falls short, giving us the encouragement not to give up. His writing is shot through with humility, not of a weak and cloying kind, but of the sort that is properly realistic and self-effacing. But this does not mean that he excuses or minimizes our human failings; rather he presents the hope that discipline, enabled by the grace of God, will bring about the hoped-for changes in our lives.

# A PROPHET FOR OUR TIMES

*I*f C. S. Lewis were alive today, he would see the fruition of trends he warned against many years ago. In 1947, in *The Abolition of Man*, he cautioned that an education based on moral relativism would have dire consequences. It would produce, he said, a generation of "men without chests," men who had lost touch with the moral law that tradition teaches us, and with their own consciences. They would be men who were unable to reason with their hearts. If he could see the current state of Western culture, he would witness the results of such an education in the explosion of degrading violence, moral chaos, the breakdown of families, and other traditional institutions. He would see as well the ethical chaos that results when we have no agreed-upon absolutes. He would see that the end result of moral relativism is the loss of human dignity.

And if he were alive today he would remind us of one of the themes that runs through all his writing: man is immortal. We are not merely trousered apes, torn between goodness and malice, who emerged by chance out of the random chaos of the universe. Instead, we are the creation of a loving and purposeful God who has placed within us an eternal soul.

All our lives, then, should be seen in the light of eternity. Our lives here are a preparation for an eternal destiny, and our daily choices are the steps by which we ascend toward glory or descend into self-chosen degradation. Heaven or Hell begins here and now.

The tragedy of our current state is made more pronounced by contemplating the glory from which we have fallen. Our dignity arises from the reality that we are created in the image of God, who will one day restore that glory which sin has tarnished. The promise is that someday we shall become truly human, taking upon ourselves the full weight of glory.

This is the message our world desperately needs to hear. If we were to believe in the God-given dignity of each human soul, how it might transform our politics, our economics, our philosophy, our entertainment, and our daily lives. If we are beings created to live for eternity, we would do well to order our lives and our society accordingly.

While we wait for eternity to dawn, our lives can demonstrate the hope that endures, even in these shadowlands. Our testimony is to a truth which is grounded in reason, not in a subjective speculation at the smorgasbord of human philosophy. Our calling is to live with joy and integrity, extending to others the dignity due them as God's creations, witnessing to how the true self can be found only in submission to God's will, not in our own self-made kingdoms of selfishness. Our trust is in a good God, whose love for us is so deep that He will use all means at His disposal to awaken us to the truth. Our reason, our imagination, the stirrings of our heart, all bear witness to His reality. Yet, though He gifts us with revelation, many of our questions will not receive the exhaustive answers we hope for. After all, His story is still unfolding and we must not forget this truth: He is not a tame lion.

# THE WRITINGS OF C. S. LEWIS

**Apologetics and Theology**

The Problem of Pain (1940)
The Case for Christianity (1942)[326]
Christian Behaviour (1943)
The Abolition of Man (1943)
Beyond Personality (1944)
George MacDonald: An Anthology (1946)
Miracles (1947)
The Weight of Glory (1949)[327]
Mere Christianity (1952)
Reflections on the Psalms (1958)
The Four Loves (1960)
The World's Last Night and Other Essays (1960)
Letters to Malcolm: Chiefly on Prayer (1964)
Christian Reflections (1967)
God in the Dock (1970)
Present Concerns (1986)
Christian Reunion (1990)

**Fiction and Poetry**

Spirits in Bondage (1919)
Dymer (1926)
The Pilgrim's Regress (1933)
Out of the Silent Planet (1938)
The Screwtape Letters (1942)

Perelandra (1943)
That Hideous Strength (1945)
The Great Divorce (1945)
The Lion, the Witch and the Wardrobe (1950)
Prince Caspian (1951)
The Voyage of the Dawn Treader (1952)
The Silver Chair (1953)
The Horse and His Boy (1954)
The Magician's Nephew (1955)
The Last Battle (1956)
Till We Have Faces (1956)
Poems (1964)
Of Other Worlds (1966)
Narrative Poems (1969)
The Dark Tower and Other Stories (1977)
Boxen (1985)

## Literary Criticism

The Allegory of Love: A Study in Medieval
    Tradition (1936)
Rehabilitations and Other Essays (1939)
The Personal Heresy (1939)
A Preface to "Paradise Lost" (1942)
Essays Presented to Charles Williams (1947)
Arthurian Torso (1948)
English Literature in the Sixteenth Century,
    Excluding Drama (1954)
Studies in Words (1960)
An Experiment in Criticism (1961)
They Asked for a Paper (1962)
The Discarded Image (1964)
Studies in Medieval and Renaissance Literature (1966)

Spenser's Images of Life (1967)
Selected Literary Essays (1969)
On Stories and Other Essays on Literature (1982)

## Autobiographical

Surprised by Joy (1955)
A Grief Observed (1961)
Letters of C. S. Lewis (1966)
Letters to An American Lady (1967)
The Letters of C. S. Lewis to Arthur Greeves (1979)
Letters to Children (1985)
Letters of C. S. Lewis and Don Giovanni Calabria (1988)
All My Road Before Me: The Diary of C. S. Lewis
    1922-1927 (1991)

# A Selective Annotated Bibliography

Michael Aeschliman, *The Restitution of Man: C. S. Lewis and the Case Against Scientism,* (Grand Rapids, MI: Eerdmans, 1983). This provocative book focuses on Lewis' attitude toward modern science.

Corbin Scott Carnell, *Bright Shadow of Reality: C. S. Lewis and the Feeling Intellect,* (Grand Rapids, MI: Eerdmans, 1974). One of the most valuable studies of C.S. Lewis, this book concentrates on his ideas about romanticism and the "longing."

Humphrey Carpenter, *The Inklings,* (Boston: Houghton Miflin, 1979). An enjoyable and informative study of Lewis and his friends.

James T. Como, ed., *C. S. Lewis at the Breakfast Table,* (New York: Harcourt, Brace and Jovanovich, 1979). A thoroughly engaging series of essays by those who knew him personally give valuable insights into Lewis the man.

Lyle Dorsett, *And God Came In,* (New York: Ballantine, 1983). A full-length study of the life of Joy Davidman.

Colin Duriez, *The C. S. Lewis Handbook,* (Grand Rapids, MI: Baker, 1990). A handbook to the people, places and themes of Lewis' life and writing.

William Griffin, *C. S. Lewis, A Dramatic Life*, (San Francisco: Harper and Row, 1986). A quirky, but very entertaining telling of Lewis' life through a series of short vignettes.

Roger Lancelyn Green and Walter Hooper, *C. S. Lewis: A Biography*, (New York: Harcourt, Brace and Jovanovich, 1974). Until that of Sayer (see below), this was the standard biography of C.S. Lewis.

Clyde Kilby and Marjorie Lamp Mead, ed., *Brothers and Friends: The Diaries of Major Warren Hamilton Lewis*, (San Francisco: Harper and Row, 1982). The diaries of Warren Lewis provide insight into the daily life of the brothers.

Michael H. Macdonald and Andrew A. Tadie, ed., *The Riddle of Joy*, (Grand Rapids, MI: Eerdmans). Essays on the life and thought of two great modern Christian thinkers: Lewis and G.K. Chesterton.

John Warwick Montgomery, ed., *Myth, Allegory and Gospel*, (Minneapolis, MN: Bethany Fellowship Publishers, 1974). Insightful essays on the fiction of Lewis, Tolkien, Chesterton, and Williams.

R. J. Reilly, *Romantic Religion*, (Athens, GA: University of Georgia Press, 1971). An academic study of romanticism in Lewis and the other Inklings.

George Sayer, *Jack: C. S. Lewis and His Times*, (San Francisco: Harper and Row, 1988). Probably the best biography of Lewis currently available.

Peter J. Schakel, *Reason and Imagination in C. S. Lewis*, (Grand Rapids, MI: Eerdmans, 1984). Although mostly a study of *Till We Have Faces*, this book also contains an interesting theory about the development of Lewis' thought.

Brian Sibley, *C. S. Lewis Through the Shadowlands*, (Grand Rapids, MI: Baker, 1994). A biography focusing on the relationship between Jack and Joy Davidman.

Andrew A. Tadie and Michael H. Macdonald, ed., *Permanent Things*, (Grand Rapids, MI: Eerdmans, 1995). A collection of essays on C.S. Lewis, G.K. Chesterton, and other writers who argued against the dehumanizing aspects of modern thought.

Andrew Walker and James Patrick, ed., *A Christian for All Christians*, (Washington D.C.: Regnery Gateway, 1992). A collection of essays on Lewis' influence and accomplishments.

William Luther White, *The Image of Man in C. S. Lewis*, (Nashville: Abingdon, 1969). A helpful study of Lewis' doctrine of man.

A. N. Wilson, *C. S. Lewis: A Biography*, (New York: Norton, 1990). A fascinating, but overly speculative biography, which contains serious errors and comes to some outrageous and unsubstantiated conclusions.

# C. S. Lewis: The Lessons of Leadership

- A leader is one who values clear thinking and the ongoing process of self-education.
- A leader puts high value on building meaningful friendships with those who can help him see beyond his own limitations.
- A leader values the insights of wise men and women who have gone before him.
- A leader is one who allows his creativity to help him see old truths in a new way.
- A leader knows that pain has much to teach us and that times of struggle are usually pregnant with insights for his life.
- A leader recognizes the danger of pride and the power of a humble spirit.
- A leader knows the power of well-chosen words to influence the mind and move the heart.
- A leader refuses to lead his life based on the changeable state of his emotions.
- A leader understands the value of humor.
- A leader enjoys life's pleasures without allowing himself to be ruled by them.
- A leader recognizes his own sinful nature and the human propensity for self-deception.
- A leader lives his life in the light of eternity.

# ENDNOTES

## C. S. Lewis: His Life

1   C. S. Lewis, *Surprised by Joy*, (New York: Harcourt, Brace Jovanovich, 1955), 237.
2   Ibid, 7.
3   Ibid, 17-18.
4   Warren Lewis, in introduction to *Letters of C. S. Lewis (revised edition)*, (New York: Harcourt, Brace and Co., 1988), 3.
5   Lewis, *Surprised by Joy*, 10.
6   Ibid, 19.
7   Ibid, 21.
8   Warren Lewis, Intro to *Letters of C. S. Lewis*, 3-4.
9   Lewis, *Surprised by Joy*, 39.
10  Roger Lancelyn Green and Walter Hooper, *C. S. Lewis: A Biography*, (New York: Harcourt, Brace and Jovanovich, 1974), 40.
11  See C. S. Lewis, *The Letters of C. S. Lewis to Arthur Greeves*, ed. by Walter Hooper (New York: Macmillan, 1979).
12  Lewis, *Surprised by Joy*, 134-135.
13  George Sayer, *Jack: C. S. Lewis and His Times*, (San Francisco: Harper and Row, 1988), 48.
14  Green and Hooper, *C. S. Lewis: A Biography*, 41-42.
15  Lewis, *Letters to Arthur Greeves*, 49.
16  Ibid, 52.
17  Ibid, 47.
18  Lewis, *Surprised by Joy*, 179.
19  Ibid., 174.
20  Ibid., 181.
21  Lewis, *Letters to Arthur Greeves*, 181.
22  Sayer, *Jack*, 73.
23  Lewis, *Letters of C. S. Lewis*, 85.
24  Lewis, *Letters to Arthur Greeves*, 221.
25  Ibid, 32-33.
26  Ibid, 136.
27  Ibid, 181.
28  Derek Brewer, "The Tutor: A Portrait" in James T. Como, *C.S. Lewis at the Breakfast Table*, (New York: Harcourt, Brace and Jovanovich, 1979), 47.
29  C. S. Lewis, *A Mind Awake*, Clyde S. Kilby, ed. (New York: Harcourt, Brace and Jovanovich, 1968), 8.
30  Warren Lewis, Introduction in *Letters*, 36.
31  Lewis, *A Mind Awake*, 8.
32  Sayer, *Jack*, 129.
33  Lewis, *Surprised by Joy*, 196.
34  C.S. Lewis, *All My Roads Before Me: The Diary of C.S. Lewis, 1922-1927*, Walter Hooper, ed. (New York: Harcourt Brace, 1991), 431.
35  Lewis, *Surprised by Joy*, 182.
36  Ibid, 211.
37  A. N. Wilson, *C. S. Lewis: A Biography*, (New York: Norton, 1990), 126-127.
38  John Bunyan, *The Pilgrim's Progress* (Grand Rapids, MI: Eerdmans, 1958), 7, 10.
39  Ibid, 10.
40  Sayer, *Jack*, 168.
41  Quote from New York Times Book Review used on back cover of Macmillan paperback edition of *Mere Christianity*.
42  Sayer, *Jack*, 173.
43  Lewis, *Letters to Arthur Greeves*, 487.

44 Sayer, *Jack*, 162.
45 Lewis, *Letters*, 355.
46 Lewis, *The Screwtape Letters*, i.
47 Warren Lewis, Intro to *Letters*, 34.
48 Warren Lewis, *Brothers and Friends: The Diaries of Major Warren Hamilton Lewis*, (San Francisco: Harper and Row, 1982), 220.
49 Lewis, *Letters*, 328.
50 C. S. Lewis, *Essays Presented to Charles Williams*, (Grand Rapids, MI: Eerdmans, 1966), ix.
51 Lewis, *Letters*, 338.
52 Ibid, 341.
53 Lewis, *Essays Presented to Charles Williams*, xiv.
54 Ibid, xiv.
55 Walter Hooper, "Oxford's Bonny Fighter" in *C. S. Lewis at the Breakfast Table*, 163.
56 Sayer, *Jack*, 187.
57 C. S. Lewis, *The World's Last Night and Other Essays* (New York: Harcourt, Brace and Jovanovich, 1960), 92.
58 Lewis, *Letters*, 382.
59 C. S. Lewis, *Poems*, (New York: Harcourt Brace and Jovanovich, 1964), 129.
60 J. R. R. Tolkien, "On Fairy Stories" in *Essays Presented to Charles Williams*, 81.
61 Lewis, *Letters*, 322.
62 Ibid, 492.
63 C. S. Lewis, *Till We Have Faces* (Grand Rapids, MI: Eerdmans, 1956), 294.
64 Lewis, *Letters*, 406.
65 Wilson, *C. S. Lewis: A Biography*, 221.
66 Sayer, *Jack*, 192.
67 Ibid., 193.
68 C. S. Lewis, *Letters to Children*, (New York: Macmillan, 1985), 52.
69 Lewis, *Letters*, 487.
70 Lewis, *Letters to Children*. (see above)
71 Lewis, *Letters*, 390.
72 C. S. Lewis, *English Literature in the Sixteenth Century, Excluding Drama*, (Oxford: Oxford University Press, 1954), 1.
73 Warren Lewis, *Brothers and Friends*, 244.
74 Letter to Jill Freud, April 5, 1955, as quoted in A. N. Wilson, *C. S. Lewis: A Biography*.
75 For complete biography on Joy, see Lyle Dorsett, *And God Came In* (New York: MacMillan, 1983)
76 Sayer, *Jack*, 212.
77 Joy Davidman, "The Longest Way Round," in *These Found the Way*, ed. D. W. Soper (Philadelphia: Westminster, 1951), 23.
78 Green and Hooper, *C. S. Lewis: A Biography*, 260.
79 Sayer, *Jack*, 221.
80 Sayer, *Jack*, 222.
81 Lewis, *Letters to Arthur Greeves*, 543.
82 Sayer, *Jack*, 224.
83 Letter to Sheldon Vanauken in *A Severe Mercy*, (San Francisco: Harper and Row, 1977), 227–228.
84 Green and Hooper, *C. S. Lewis: A Biography*, 270.
85 Lewis, *Letters*, 482.
86 C. S. Lewis, *A Grief Observed*, (New York: Bantam, 1976), 6.
87 Ibid, 4.
88 Ibid., 53–54.
89 Warren Lewis, introduction to *Letters*, 46.
90 Green and Hooper, *C. S. Lewis: A Biography*, 306.
91 C. S. Lewis, *The Silver Chair*, (New York: Macmillan, 1953), 19.
92 Lewis, *Surprised by Joy*, 7.
93 Ibid, 17-18.
94 Lewis, *Surprised by Joy*, 181.
95 Lewis, *The Mind Awake*, 23.
96 C. S. Lewis, *Mere Christianity*, (New York: Macmillan, 1952), 120.
97 C. S. Lewis, *The Problem of Pain*, (New York: Macmillan, 1962), 145, 148.
98 C. S. Lewis, *The Weight of Glory*, (New York: Macmillan, 1962), 16-17.
99 C. S. Lewis, *Miracles*, (New York: Macmillan, 1947), 96-97.
100 Lewis, *The World's Last Night and Other Essays*, 26.

101 Lewis, *Miracles*, 93.
102 C. S. Lewis, *Christian Reflections*, (Grand Rapids, MI: Eerdmans, 1967), 171.
103 C. S. Lewis, *Letters to Malcolm*, (New York: Harcourt, Brace and Jovanovich 1963), 75.
104 C. S. Lewis, *The Four Loves*, (New York: Harcourt, Brace and Jovanovich, 1960), 176.
105 Lewis, *Letters*, 409.
106 Lewis, *Mere Christianity*, 38.
107 Lewis, *The Problem of Pain*, 40.
108 Lewis, *Mere Christianity*, 118.
109 C. S. Lewis, *Perelandra*, (New York: Macmillan, 1944), 116.
110 Colin Duriez, *The C. S. Lewis Handbook*, (Grand Rapids: Baker, 1990), 72.
111 C. S. Lewis, *The Last Battle*, (New York: Macmillan, 1956), 133.
112 Lewis, *Miracles*, 112.
113 Lewis, *Mere Christianity*, 55-56.
114 Ibid, 60.
115 Ibid, 62.
116 Lewis, *The Silver Chair*, 17.
117 C. S. Lewis, *God in the Dock*, (Grand Rapids, MI: Eerdmans, 1970), 160.
118 Lewis, *Mere Christianity*, 53.
119 Ibid, 135.
120 Lewis, *The World's Last Night*, 18.
121 Lewis, *Mere Christianity*, 123.
122 Lewis, *Christian Reflections*, 42.
123 Lewis, *God in the Dock*, 101.
124 Ibid, 111-112.
125 Lewis, *The Problem of Pain*, 93.
126 Ibid, 105.
127 Ibid.
128 C. S. Lewis, *Letters to An American Lady*, (Grand Rapids, MI: Eerdmans, 1967), 20.
129 Lewis, *Letters*, 406.
130 Lewis, *God in the Dock*, 29.
131 Ibid, 52.
132 Lewis, *Miracles*, 3.
133 Ibid, 60-61.
134 Ibid, 61.
135 Lewis, *Mere Christianity*, 20.
136 Ibid, 53.
137 Ibid, 54.
138 Lewis, *God in the Dock*, 66.
139 Lewis, *Miracles*, 139.
140 Lewis, *The Allegory of Love*, (Oxford: Oxford University Press, 1938), 47.
141 Lewis, *Letters to Arthur Greeves*, 288.
142 Lewis, *God in the Dock*, 66-67.
143 C. S. Lewis, *George MacDonald: An Anthology*, (New York: Macmillan, 1946), 16-17.
144 Lewis, *God in the Dock*, 67.
145 Lewis, *The Silver Chair*, 212.
146 Lewis, *Letters to Arthur Greeves*, 476.
147 C. S. Lewis, *The Abolition of Man*, (New York: Macmillan, 1965), 29.
148 C. S. Lewis, *On Stories*, (New York: Harcourt, Brace and Jovanovich, 1966), 34.
149 Lewis, *Mere Christianity*, 75.
150 Lewis, *Letters to Arthur Greeves*, 447.
151 Lewis, *On Stories*, 42.
152 C. S. Lewis, *Prince Caspian*, (New York: Macmillan, 1951), 117.
153 Lewis, *Mere Christianity*, 161.
154 Green and Hooper, *C. S. Lewis: A Biography*, 292.
155 Lewis, *Surprised by Joy*, 10.
156 Ibid, 191.
157 Lewis, *Letters to Malcolm*, 12
158 C. S. Lewis, "Introduction" to St. Athanasius, *On the Incarnation of the Word*, Crestwood, NY: St.
    Vladimirs Orthodox Seminary Press, 1993), 4.
159 C. S. Lewis, *An Experiment in Criticism*, (Cambridge: Cambridge University Press, 1961), 2.
160 Lewis, *Letters to Arthur Greeves*, 438.

161  Lewis, Ibid, 94.
162  Lewis, *An Experiment in Criticism*, 141.
163  Green and Hooper, *C. S. Lewis: A Biography*, 142.
164  Lewis, *The Four Loves*, 103
165  Lewis, *Letters to Arthur Greeves*, 477.
166  Lewis, *The Four Loves*, 113.
167  Ibid, 98.
168  C. S. Lewis, *Present Concerns*, (London: Collins, 1986), 20.
169  C. S. Lewis, *Selected Literary Essays*, (Cambridge: Cambridge University Press, 1969), 99.
170  Lewis, *The Four Loves*, 96-97.
171  C. S. Lewis, *The Magician's Nephew*, (New York: Macmillan, 1955), 106.
172  C. S. Lewis, *Reflections on the Psalms*, (New York: Macmillan, 1958), 90.
173  Lewis, *The Problem of Pain*, 136-137.
174  Lewis, *On Stories*, 153.
175  Lewis, *Miracles*, 32.
176  Lewis, *The Screwtape Letters*, 52.
177  Ibid, ix.
178  Lewis, *Selected Literary Essays*, 12.
179  Ibid, 13.
180  Lewis, *Christian Reflections*, 82-93.
181  Lewis, *Surprised by Joy*, 207-208.
182  Lewis, *The Abolition of Man*, 41.
183  Lewis, *Letters*, 204.
184  C. S. Lewis, *Studies in Words*, (Cambrdige: Cambridge University Press, 1960), 150.
185  Cited by Christopher Derrick in "C. S. Lewis: Against the Cult of Culture," *The Times* (London): Apr. 28 1973.
186  Lewis, *Letters*, 269.
187  Cited in Michael Aeschliman, *The Restitution of Man*, (Grand Rapids, MI: Eerdmans, 1983), 5.
188  Lewis, *God in the Dock*, 338.
189  Aeschliman, 5.
190  Lewis, *Mere Christianity*, 21.
191  Lewis, *Miracles*, 36.
192  Lewis, *Christian Reflections*, 73.
193  Ibid.
194  Ibid.
195  Ibid, 75.
196  Ibid.
197  Ibid, 78.
198  Lewis, *Miracles*, 33.
199  Aeschliman, *The Restitution of Man*, 48.
200  Green and Hooper, *C. S. Lewis: A Biography*, 173.
201  Lewis, *The Weight of Glory*, 72.
202  C. S. Lewis, *The Voyage of the Dawn Treader*, (New York: Macmillan, 1952), 180.
203  Lewis, *Weight of Glory*, 71.
204  Lewis, *The Abolition of Man*, 3.
205  Lewis, *Miracles*, 135.
206  Lewis, *English Literature in the Sixteenth Century*, 322.
207  Lewis, *Mere Christianity*, 69.
208  Ibid, 69.
209  Lewis, *The Abolition of Man*, 88.
210  Lewis, *Mere Christianity*, 73.
211  Ibid, 77.
212  Lewis, *Mere Christianity*, 77.
213  G.K. Chesterton, *Tremendous Trifles* (New York: Dodd, Mead and Co., 1917), 14.
214  Ibid, 125.
215  Lewis, *God in the Dock*, 172-176.
216  Lewis, *The World's Last Night*, 25.
217  Lewis, *Christian Reflections*, 42-43.
218  Ibid.
219  Lewis, *Mere Christianity*, 123-124.
220  Ibid, 128.

221 Ibid, 130.
222 Lewis, *The Screwtape Letters*, 39.
223 Lewis, *The World's Last Night*, 109.
224 Lewis, *Mere Christianity*, 123.
225 Lewis, *Letters*, 411-12.
226 Lewis, *Letters*, 99.
227 Lewis, *Letters*, 421.
228 Lewis, *Letters*, 116.
229 Lewis, *Letters*, 60.
230 Lewis, *Poems*, 120.
231 Lewis, *The World's Last Night*, 3
232 Lewis, *Christian Reflections*, 144.
233 Lewis, *The World's Last Night*, 4-5.
234 Lewis, *Letters to Malcolm*, 63.
235 Ibid, 16.
236 Ibid, 23.
237 Lewis, *The Magician's Nephew*, 134.
238 Lewis, *Letters to An American Lady*, 110.
239 C. S. Lewis, *A Preface to Paradise Lost*, (Oxford: Oxford University Press, 1942), 70-71.
240 Lewis, *Mere Christianity*, 53-54.
241 Lewis, *A Preface to Paradise Lost*, 96-97.
242 Lewis, *The Problem of Pain*, 75-76.
243 Lewis, *The World's Last Night*, 89.
244 William White, *The Image of Man in C. S. Lewis*, (Nashville, TN: Abingdon, 1969), 131.
245 Lewis, *Mere Christianity*, 59.
246 Lewis, *The Screwtape Letters*, 56.
247 Lewis, *Letters*, 365.
248 Lewis, *Mere Christianity*, 51.
249 Lewis, *The Screwtape Letters*, 2.
250 Jeffrey Barton Russell, *Mephistopheles: The Devil in the Modern World*, (Ithica, NY: Cornell University Press, 1986).
251 Lewis, *The Problem of Pain*, 134.
252 Lewis, *A Preface to Paradise Lost*, 96-97.
253 Ibid, 99.
254 Lewis, *The Problem of Pain*, 127.
255 Ibid, 123.
256 Lewis, *The Screwtape Letters*, ix.
257 C. S. Lewis, *The Great Divorce*, (New York: Macmillan, 1945), 72-73.
258 Lewis, *Present Concerns*, 54-55.
259 Lewis, *The Screwtape Letters*, 41.
260 Lewis, *The Allegory of Love*, 15.
261 Lewis, *Mere Christianity*, 76.
262 Ibid, 94-95.
263 Lewis, *Letters to Malcolm*, 88-89.
264 Lewis, *God in the Dock*, 318.
265 Lewis, *The Weight of Glory*, 3-4.
266 Lewis, *Christian Reflections*, 7.
267 Ibid, 15.
268 Ibid, 25.
269 Ibid, 23.
270 Ibid, 36.
271 Lewis, *English Literature in the Sixteenth Century*, 529.
272 Lewis, *The World's Last Night*, 80.
273 Lewis, *An Experiment in Criticism*, 19.
274 Lewis, *The Weight of Glory*, 109.
275 Lewis, *Letters*, 414.
276 Ibid, 473.
277 Lewis, *Present Concerns*, 17.
278 Ibid, 73-74.
279 Lewis, *God in the Dock*, 199.
280 Lewis, *The Great Divorce*, 92.

281 Lewis, *Mere Christianity*, 89.
282 Lewis, *Letters*, 438.
283 Lewis, *Mere Christianity*, 97.
284 Ibid, 101.
285 Ibid, 116.
286 Lewis, *The Four Loves*, 41-42.
287 Lewis, *Letters*, 429.
288 Lewis, *Miracles*, 52.
289 C. S. Lewis, *The Horse and His Boy*, (New York: Macmillan, 1954), 193.
290 Lewis, *Mere Christianity*, 110-111.
291 Ibid, 108-109.
292 Ibid, 114.
293 Lewis, *Letters to Arthur Greeves*, 339.
294 Lewis, *The Four Loves*, 180.
295 Lewis, *Mere Christianity*, 113.
296 Lewis, *Christian Reflections*, 14.
297 Lewis, *Letters*, 422.
298 Lewis, *Letters to Malcolm*, 91.
299 Ibid., 90.
300 The essay is "Sacramental Mysticism in Chesterton and Lewis" in *CSL: The Bulletin of the New York C. S. Lewis Society*, 21, No. 1 (November 1989): 1-2. I was led to this article by the very fine essay "C. S. Lewis Celebrates 'Patches of Godlight'" by George Musacchio in *Permanent Things*, (Grand Rapids, MI: Eerdmans, 1995), 82-90. I am indebted to Musacchio's article for many of the insights of this chapter.
301 Lewis, *Letters to Arthur Greeves*, 80.
302 Lewis, *Surprised by Joy*, 152.
303 Lewis, *Letters to Malcolm*, 90.
304 Sayer, *Jack*, 53.
305 Lewis, *Present Concerns*, 51-52.
306 Lewis, *God in the Dock*, 216.
307 Lewis, *Mere Christianity*, 172.
308 Ibid, 117.
309 Ibid, 161.
310 C. S. Lewis, *The Voyage of the Dawn Treader*, (New York: Macmillan, 1952), 75-76; 90-91.
311 Lewis, *Mere Christianity*, 171.
312 Ibid, 174.
313 Lewis, *Letters to An American Lady*, 81.
314 Lewis, *God in the Dock*, 150.
315 C. S. Lewis, *Out of the Silent Planet*, (New York: Macmillan, 1938), 140.
316 Lewis, *The Great Divorce*, 104.
317 Lewis, *Till We Have Faces*, 279.
318 Lewis, *Letters to An American Lady*, 119-120.
319 Lewis, *The Last Battle*, 170.
320 Lewis, *Mere Christianity*, 118.
321 Lewis, *The Weight of Glory*, 16-17.
322 Lewis, *The Problem of Pain*, 147-148.
323 Lewis, *The Last Battle*, 173.
324 *Mere Christianity, The Screwtape Letters*.
325 Lewis, *A Preface to Paradise Lost*, 100.
326 Originally published in Britain as "Broadcast Talks"
327 Originally published in Britain as "Transposition and Other Addresses"